SHINING LIKE STARS

Shining Like Stars

Living Boldly in Love and Conviction

JENNI BUTZ

ISBN-13: 978-0-9992884-6-7 (print book)
ISBN-13: 978-0-9992884-7-4 (ebook)

Cover design by O'Daniel Designs

Printed in the United States of America

Legacy ONE AUTHORS

Kirkland, WA

LegacyOneAuthors.com

Dedication

To Tony,
who makes me a better writer
and a better person

Contents

Acknowledgments

The Pleiades constellation is also referred to as Seven Sisters, and I love the image that conjures up for me: women sticking together to speak life to one another so we can shine. That's how this book was birthed. How can I possibly thank all the women in my life who have fed into the work produced here? The women who gave me skills, resources, and opportunities to learn and flex my leadership muscles started me on a path to doing what God created me to do. Thank you, Vicki, Sherry, and Kristi. My decades-long friendships with my EPIC chicks has given me confidence to live out loud in the way I was created to live. Thank you, Jules, Colleen, Heather, Lisa, and Mel. Competent and kind professional women have coached me, challenged me, hired me, and worked with me, allowing me to shine light into the libraries, conference rooms, churches, and stages where I work. Thank you, Kirsten, Gazala, Christina Marie, and Karen. Thank you doesn't begin to cover the profound gratitude I have for my mom's love and support as long as I've been alive. She shines so beautifully in her way, and she encourages me to shine in mine. Thank you, Mom. There have been amazing women in my life over the years who have let me share God's Word and invest in them, and I have learned so much in the process! Thank you, Mary Kay, Cat, Emmalyn, Kaito, Carolyn, and Rochelle. I have loved watching you discover the light you're meant to shine in the world! All of these women have made writing this book possible. Thank you for your hard questions, your stubborn love, and your confidence that I could do it!

Shining Like Stars:

Living Boldly in Love and Conviction

*O*ne of my favorite quotes of all time is by 19th century French writer and philosopher Emile Zola:

> *If you ask me what I came into this world to do,*
> *I will tell you: I came to live out loud.*

I've learned throughout my life that living out loud isn't the same as living loudly. Living out loud means living boldly, but not being offensive. It means knowing who we are regardless of how our circumstances or relationships change over time. But sometimes we forget.

All through my adolescent years and into my 30s, depression was a constant companion. Teen angst often spiraled into long crying jags and debilitating and cruel inner dialogues. As an adult, with a job, then a marriage and a child, I was able to function when necessary, but there were seasons when I was crippled by depression so that socializing and leisure activities were perfunctory at best and impossible on bad days.

Throughout this period of my life, I attended church and Bible studies, but I simply could not access the power of the words in the book I'd come to love so much. Those very words became a foundation so that the bottom would not entirely fall out from under me in my life, but I wasn't aware of the transformative power they could bring. Or that they were transforming me while I was unaware.

In my early 30s, I attended a Christian women's conference with some friends, where hundreds of other women in the area gathered for worship and to hear teaching on a variety of subjects. To this day I couldn't tell you who put on the conference or why I went. But there was a breakout session on depression for women who were helping other women through it. I felt compelled to go more to understand my own struggle than to be equipped to help others.

It was life-changing. Not only did I finally have a name for what I'd been battling most of my life; I now had specific Scriptures to memorize and use when I was tempted to beat myself up incessantly and question my very worth and purpose for being alive.

That night during the worship service, God gave me a vision of me standing at the edge of a cliff, looking down at a deep gorge. I knew that precipice was my depression and signified the temptation I had felt to end my life at my lowest moments. God showed me that cliff and said to my spirit, "You will never go there again." Just like that. Not that I would never struggle again. Not that I would never be sad. Not that I would never doubt. But that I would never go to the depths I had gone to before. It's the closest I have been in my life to instantaneous healing. And for the past 20 years, I have struggled, I have been sad, and I have doubted. But I have never despaired or questioned in the same way.

That encounter seemed to have the effect of unleashing all the Scripture I have studied in my life to give it new transformative power as I've matured and become more of who God created me to be. When I'm tempted to question my worth or my purpose, I'm reminded that I am fearfully and wonderfully made, a child of God who is wildly and profoundly loved. I have specific gifts to use to help people. God is pleased with me. These are the foundational truths I go back to when I need to remind myself, or the enemy who accuses me, that I belong to God and that He who is in me is greater than he who is in the world. Feelings need to be acknowledged for what they may reveal, but they are not the boss of me. Jesus is!

As I've assimilated more and more Scripture into my head and heart, and as God has done His work in me over the years, I remember how to live out loud. I'm reminded how to shine for God in a dark world. I recall words of truth, love, and comfort to lift me up toward my ultimate purpose in life: to know and give glory to God.

Knowing who God is and knowing what He says about us are central to living the Christian life. Being sure of and embracing our true identity is crucial to living out loud and to shining like stars.

My question to you as we begin this journey is this: *Do you know who you are?*

Once that question has been posed and considered, myriad others present themselves and are related to the answer.

Consider the following:

If I'm not sure of my identity, how can I give my best to the world?

If my identity is in the wrong things, who am I when my circumstances change?

As a woman of faith, how do I identify and claim my unique identity as a child of God without comparing myself—both favorably and unfavorably—to people around me?

How can I cling to my foundational identity while still changing and growing as God's Spirit transforms me in various seasons of life?

Finally, how can knowing my identity, based on what Scripture tells me, enable me to represent Jesus well as I interact with the world around me? How can I shine brightly in a society that doesn't embrace Christian values and may even belittle me for my convictions?

Through almost 30 years of studying Scripture, teaching it to others, and helping women gain tools to understand and engage with the Bible so they can teach others, I've seen a growing correlation between strength of conviction and knowledge of what the Bible says. I've said many times that simply reading Scripture won't guarantee that you will grow in your relationship with God and have a powerful witness for Him, but NOT knowing Scripture guarantees that you won't.

My recent growing passion has been to help women connect the dots to see that not only is ALL Scripture God-breathed and useful for teaching, rebuking, correcting, and training (2 Timothy 3:16-17), but that it's also accessible. To everyone. Studying the Bible is not only a scholarly pursuit for the academically minded. It's for the simple-minded, the creative, the athletic, the passionate, the domestic, the corporate, the scientific, the social, and the nature-loving children God created to know Him and love Him. And with knowledge comes freedom and conviction to live the life we were created to live.

Textbook authors Andreas J. Köstenberger and Richard D. Patterson give compelling reasons for every Christian to be intentional about reading and understanding the Bible:

> *Why would we want to take the time and exert the effort to learn to interpret Scripture correctly?...because we are seekers of truth and because we realize that truth sets free while error enslaves...There is an even more powerful motivation, however: embarking on the quest for accurate biblical interpretation out of our love for God, his Word, and his people...Rather than being exclusively, or even primarily, a scholarly pursuit, interpretation is required of every believer...For this reason, we all should assume responsibility for our spiritual growth and make every effort to grow in our ability to handle God's Word accurately and with increasing skill.* [1]

We cannot live out what we believe if we don't know what we believe. And if we, as Christians, don't derive our convictions from Scripture, we must be honest about identifying alternative sources which may or may not corroborate tenets found in Scripture. Do our convictions come from our favorite sitcom characters? Do we base our values on what we've learned in science classes? On observations in society? And the convictions we may collect often begin with our identity, since that is the one prevailing piece of foundational information we carry with us throughout our lives. It's also often the one area where we are most susceptible to believing false information coming from negative or erroneous sources.

Our identity is only one of many convictions or values that inform our lives as we make decisions and pursue a Christian life. Out of identity flow attitudes and behaviors. An example of one practical and applicable passage from the Bible comes from the book of Ephesians and lends itself fairly easily to forming convictions about our everyday lives:

> *Do not let any unwholesome talk come out of your mouths, but only what is helpful for building others up according to their needs, that it may benefit those who listen.*
>
> (Ephesians 4:29)

Most Christians would agree that it is important for us to speak positively and encouragingly to one another and that it is something we should strive to do more frequently. However, how these guidelines manifest themselves in our lives may vary from person to person. Some will claim a conviction to no longer swear like a sailor. (No offense, sailors…) Some will make an earnest attempt to be more encouraging to coworkers or family members. And others will resolve to simply say less in general. What we all have in common is the fact that once these words are read and internalized, we can no longer claim ignorance of them. Therefore, we can move in the direction that the Holy Spirit guides us, armed with truth that informs our words.

Why Stars?

So what does all of this have to do with stars? Look at the following verses, which will serve as guidelines for our efforts together:

> *Do everything without grumbling or arguing, so that you may become blameless and pure, "children of God without fault in a warped and crooked generation." Then you will shine among them like stars in the sky as you hold firmly to the word of life...*
>
> (Philippians 2:14-16)

This translation is from the NIV Bible. Other translations of verse 15 use the word *lights* instead of *stars*, but the impact can be seen in both. The overarching message in these verses is that our role, as those who love and follow Jesus, is to shine brightly in the middle of a world— a society, a neighborhood, a workplace, a family—that one might consider hostile or immoral.

And in the same way that stars can be seen to twinkle most brightly in a very dark sky, we can illuminate God's character and His love for this world by knowing who we are, boldly living out our biblical convictions, and speaking truth to those who see the difference in our lives. Even as Paul is using figurative language by comparing Christ followers to stars or bright lights, I see several facts about stars that can inspire us in our journeys:

1) **Stars shine.** We are called to shine—to be light in the darkness that surrounds us.

2) **Stars orbit yet remain fixed.** We are created to orbit around our Creator—God Almighty—as we then remain fixed in our convictions and let the world's messages swirl around us.

3) **Stars change over time.** Followers of Jesus are dynamic and called to become more and more like Jesus as the Holy Spirit does His work to change us.

4) **Stars can flare up and burn out.** We all flame out, burn out, and lash out; sin is crouching at our door and wants to master us. But how does this change the way we shine?

5) **Stars remain in constellations.** There are abundant examples in Scripture encouraging us to remain in community with other believers along with examples of what that should look like.

The birth, existence, transformation, and death of stars can teach us some things about following Jesus. And much of this knowledge and wisdom comes from Scripture. My prayer for you is that you will be convinced, if not convicted, to shine brightly out of assurances that the Holy Spirit reveals to you from the Bible. Without that foundation, it is far more challenging to know, articulate, and live by our beliefs. Jesus said, *"If you hold to my teaching, you are really my disciples. Then you will know the truth, and the truth will set you free"* (John 8:31-32). Jesus Himself is the truth; He's also God. When we immerse ourselves in His presence and read His Word, we will be changed: free to speak and live out truths that were previously vague and tentative for us. When that happens, we're free to listen to others' opinions without feeling threatened. We're released from the pressure to compare ourselves to others. Service to others becomes more natural, and shame is transformed into confession and forgiveness.

Doesn't that sound glorious?

Positive attitude without complaining or arguing. Illuminating and encouraging others toward truth. Freedom and spiritual transformation even when I fail. And it all starts with opening the most important book in history. You can do this! Even if, as a friend of mine said about herself once, you don't know what you don't know, you can learn and grow in this area like in any other area of life.

Remember this tune from childhood?

> Twinkle, twinkle, little star,
> How I wonder what you are!
> Up above the world so high,
> Like a diamond in the sky.

Did you know that there are multiple verses to this little ditty? This verse is particularly relevant as we begin our discussion on stars and their connection to our spiritual journeys:

> Then the traveler in the dark
> Thanks you for your tiny spark;
> He could not see where to go,
> If you did not twinkle so.

We can shine brightly to light the way for our fellow travelers on this earth to find Jesus. We can ignite curiosity and engage the world boldly when we have a firm grasp of our convictions that comes from His unfailing and unchanging Word.

Questions for Discussion or Application:

+ If you have ever been to a planetarium or taken an astronomy class, what do you remember about the experience?

+ Reread Philippians 2:14-16. These are the theme verses for the following chapters. What strikes you most about the verses? What word(s) or phrase(s) are you most curious about? Which are challenging?

Chapter 1

See The Universe

*I*f we look up from earth on a clear, dark night, we can see countless lights twinkling in the black expanse above us. There may be a bright moon hovering fat and full near the horizon, or simply millions of seemingly random dots sprinkled across the sky. Some of us remember school field trips to the planetarium to learn about the constellations and their stories from ancient civilizations. You may have become skilled at spotting Orion's belt or the Big and Little Dippers. I remember being awakened in the middle of the night as a kid in Indiana so my parents could take my brother and me out to see the Northern Lights. I have a vague recollection of standing in the grass in my nightgown, rubbing my eyes, and wondering why I was awake. I wish I had known how special the sight was at the time!

The night sky, away from city lights, with even the most novice-level telescope, reveals stars, planets, and other mysteries of the universe. Our home planet Earth is located in the Milky Way Galaxy, and we, along with the other planets in our solar system, revolve around the sun. We turn on our axis and continue with amazing regularity on our orbit around the sun at the perfect distance to sustain life and our seasons. When we look out into space, the lights we see may be planets, stars, meteors, comets, or asteroids. But stars capture our imagination in a special way. They remind us of diamonds. Of sequins. They seem to sparkle and twinkle in a romantic and magical way. Why is this? And what are they?

A star is a luminous ball of gas, mostly hydrogen and helium, held together by its own gravity. Nuclear fusion reactions in its core support the star against gravity and produce photons and heat, as well as small amounts of heavier elements.[1] That's certainly more scientific than magical, but they look so pretty from earth! And they are just one of many kinds of celestial bodies that inhabit the space above and around us. I make no claims at knowing or understanding a fraction of what's out there, but I'd like to use some of what I do know to point us to the One who designed and created it all.

There was a theory among very early civilizations that the earth was spherical instead of the shape of a flat disc. However, most educated societies believed that the earth was flat and that we were the center of things that revolved around us, despite some evidence from ancient writings and nautical observations. (Doesn't that say a lot about human nature?) In the 16th century Polish astronomer and mathematician Nicolaus Copernicus posited the theory that the earth might not, in fact, be in the center of things, but that it might orbit around the sun. These findings were confirmed and were controversial for many years, until science and general human understanding could catch up with early thinkers. This led to expanded exploration and trade as leaders shed their fear of ships falling into the abyss off the side of the disc-shaped planet.

The 16th century also saw the invention of the telescope and the discovery of the laws of motion and gravity, which greatly expanded our understanding of the universe and of our place in it. In the 21st century we can't imagine fearing that a cruise ship will fall off the earth, thinking that the sun is revolving around us, or believing in celestial, magical lights of the gods. We know, even if we don't have a full grasp of the concepts and details, that stars are made of hydrogen and helium and that the sun is the center of the solar system around which our spherical planet orbits. Not only that, we have confidence that, despite what cursory understanding we may have of gravity, tubes of metal can lift off the ground and fly through the air at hundreds of miles per hour with loads of cargo and passengers. We know what Mars looks like. We are familiar with the make-up and surface of the moon and understand perfectly what is happening when we see a sliver or a white full circle in the sky at night.

We know all of it and it gives us confidence to move and work and travel and live. We know what we believe and that knowledge informs our conscious and unconscious decisions.

Why is our faith any different?

Why do we compare ourselves to others and feel insignificant or unlovable when we know that God loves us and created us with a purpose?

Why do we so often shrink back from robust dialogue with friends and colleagues who sincerely want to know more about our faith and the God we love and follow?

Why do we falter when asked where we stand on social or moral issues?

Why do we trust our pastors and Bible study leaders to inform us of God's position and the history of His people rather than delving into it for ourselves?

I'm convinced that it's because we don't consistently and intentionally apply ourselves to learning and understanding our faith and relationship with God through the Bible. We see what faith looks like shining in others and we may envy another person's boldness and sense of self, but we haven't studied and grasped the foundational truths of our faith. Truths that could set us free and make us shine.

I've experienced this transformation myself, and it's not overstating it to say that it's completely changed my life.

I grew up in church, singing in choir, attending youth group functions, and regularly participating in Sunday School. In college, I met some women who helped me see the importance of sharing my faith with others and studying the Bible together. I still hadn't established much of an individual discipline for reading Scripture on my own, but I could see that it was more practical than I had originally thought. And it was the first time in my spiritual life when I was involved in Bible studies and started to understand what people talked about when they said that they had had their "quiet time" that morning. I saw how the Bible was put together and started to understand the historical context as well as the personal relevance.

When I got a job as a teacher, becoming involved in church life and volunteering with Christian athletes at the high school where I taught, I found myself surrounded by people who looked and acted and spoke the way I imagined good Christian people should. But I wasn't confident about living out what I was learning about God in a way that was relevant and authentic.

When my husband and I got married, we had a bumpy first few years. God showed us His goodness by putting us in a small church with passionate, authentic people who helped us find our footing by anchoring us to God's love and truth. We were both involved in small groups that talked about how the Bible applied to our lives, and we all encouraged each other to share what God was saying to us in our times alone with Him. I developed an affinity for studying the Bible and started to lead and write my own material with groups of women.

It was this group of people and our common need for and growing love of the Bible that sustained us when we got some very difficult news.

Just after our son Charlie's 8th birthday, we went to the doctor because he wasn't feeling well. By the evening of that day, we had been admitted to Children's Hospital in Seattle with the diagnosis of Acute Lymphoblastic Leukemia. Cancer. I have yet to encounter a mother who isn't quick to admit that her greatest fear is something like this happening to her child. Charlie's cancer was "the best kind" for a kid his age, we were told, but the diagnosis and subsequent treatments were difficult, to say the least.

The morning after we were admitted, I woke up to the sound of machines humming and beeping in our unfamiliar environment, and I did what I had conditioned myself to do over the past several years: I opened my Bible. I had been reading through the Bible in a year, and I opened my chart to the next day's reading, 1 Kings 17, and I began to read:

> *After this the son of the woman, the mistress of the house, became ill. And his illness was so severe that there was no breath left in him. And she said to Elijah, "What have you against me, O man of God? You have come to me to bring my sin to remembrance and to cause the death of my son!" And he said to her, "Give me your son." And he took him from her arms and carried him up into the upper chamber where he lodged, and laid him on his own bed. And he cried to the Lord, "O Lord my God, have you brought calamity even upon the widow with whom I sojourn, by killing her son?" Then he stretched himself upon the child three times and cried to the Lord, "O Lord my God,*

let this child's life come into him again." And the Lord listened to the voice of Elijah. And the life of the child came into him again, and he revived. And Elijah took the child and brought him down from the upper chamber into the house and delivered him to his mother. And Elijah said, "See, your son lives." And the woman said to Elijah, "Now I know that you are a man of God, and that the word of the Lord in your mouth is truth."

(1 Kings 17:17-24)

I could only read that far before asking God, "What does this mean? Does this mean Charlie is going to die? Does it mean he's going to be ok?"

In no time at all I sensed God say very clearly to me, "It means that I knew you would be here today. I knew how may days behind you were in your reading schedule. It means I'm here with you." Reading this particular passage on this particular day in these very particular circumstances was not a coincidence. And it brought me profound comfort over the course of the following 3½ years of chemotherapy, doctor visits, and all that comes with cancer. I was repeatedly reminded that God had spoken to me in my desperation through a section of Scripture written thousands of years before any of us were born.

Charlie's cancer was cured and he went on to thrive in middle school and the first couple years of high school. Good grades, great friends, active in youth group, and a new ability to participate in sports and activities that most of his peers had taken for granted the years he was sick.

Then his junior year of high school, we discovered that Charlie was smoking pot. This fact alone wasn't too shocking as I had taught high school for a number of years, and I didn't think that we would be spared our share of teen challenges and emerge from those years unscathed. But I wasn't prepared for the rapidly escalating drug use and erratic, addictive, risky behavior that ensued. I remember the day that I stopped telling Charlie to avoid certain boys who were a bad influence, because I realized that *he* was the bad influence!

Things became so dire and we were so worried about Charlie that the second week of his senior year of high school, we had two transport agents come at 4 am to put him in a white SUV to go to the airport and catch a flight to take him to a rehab facility for boys in the middle of the Utah desert. My husband and I gently shook him in the dark and said, "Charlie, it's time to wake up now. You're going to a new school today. We love you. Please be cooperative."

Charlie spent the following 11 months in individual and group therapy sessions, working hard, going to school, and growing in physical and emotional strength. We only talked to him twice a month for a family therapy call. Letters were exchanged every week, and we all experienced profound changes that are still with us today. It wasn't the senior year any of us anticipated, but once again, we found ourselves doing whatever was necessary to keep Charlie alive.

In the year leading up to Charlie's departure, I was reading through the book of Haggai. It's a short book—only two chapters—and not one that I had spent a lot of time studying. But there I was again, reading through every book of the Bible, sometimes in a year, sometimes it took longer, and God spoke to me again through a rather obscure bit of the Old Testament.

Here's the passage that God lit up for me:

> *This is what the Lord Almighty says: "In a little while I will once more shake the heavens and the earth, the sea and the dry land. I will shake all nations, and what is desired by all nations will come, and I will fill this house with glory," says the Lord Almighty. "The silver is mine and the gold is mine," declares the Lord Almighty. "The glory of this present house will be greater than the glory of the former house," says the Lord Almighty. "And in this place I will grant peace," declares the Lord Almighty.*
>
> (Haggai 2:6-9)

This tiny little book of only two chapters was illuminated for me so powerfully that it made my heart race. I felt like God was speaking to me, saying, "Jenni, I will fill this house with my glory and my peace, and your family will experience my presence here." We had just moved into a new, smaller house, thinking that it would be easier to keep tabs on Charlie once we discovered his drug use. I was convinced that this passage on this day was God's promise to me that Charlie would turn around and that his drug use would stop and our family would be happy and whole again.

Then things got worse.

I kept going back to the passage, asking God, "Are you sure, Lord? Was this for me? Am I making this up?" I had a consistent assurance that this was, in fact, for me, but the timeline and vision were less clear. Then we sent Charlie away. When he returned almost a year later, I asked God, "Now, Lord? Now you will bring peace to our house, right?"

Within three weeks after Charlie's return from rehab he was sneaking out in the middle of the night, smoking pot, and hanging with his old buddies.

Not yet.

When Charlie left for college I did a little research into the timeline of the passage in Haggai to discover that it was *years* after this passage that the temple was completed and God's glory filled the temple. *Years.* I began to understand that not only had God reassured me over and over that He was in control of and had good plans for our family, but that He had also done some miraculous work in my marriage when I wasn't looking for it. God was bringing peace and His glory into our house; it just wasn't the way I anticipated or prayed for.

The bottom line in both of these stories is that God's Word was an unchanging, foundational anchor in my life in general, AND it was a living, active part of my growth in very specific and difficult circumstances.

God's Word is true in general AND it is true very specifically.

We experience the knowledge of the truth of Scripture AND we experience God emotionally as we read.

For most of us, when we first understood that we were sinners, having fallen short of the standard that a perfect, loving, and holy God has established, our natural response was to be grateful and humbled, accepting the gift of salvation through the death and resurrection of Jesus. For many of us, the emotions that come with a commitment to Christ are then enough to sustain and energize us into making some relationship or morality changes.

Time to go to church. Change vocabulary from F-bombs to *thankyouJesus*. Peace flows like a river, and our spirits are less altered by, well, spirits.

But emotions aren't enough for transformation and long-term soul change. Chasing sensational experiences and relying on initial information from early days as a Christ-follower equates to attempting to replicate the excitement of the first few dates of a meaningful relationship. I won't be inspired to serve and love another person by remembering something that I learned about him decades ago. And I'm no more likely to share Christ with others and stand firm in my convictions if I only have a cursory, past knowledge of who He is. Powerful relationships with people are like our relationship with God: they are richer and more vibrant when the encounters are fresh.

I talk to many women who have spiritual questions, passions, or doubts, but they aren't sure how to speak up confidently and declare foundational truths. So they second-guess decisions or change their minds about issues because other people make compelling arguments or are more persuasive and articulate.

There is tremendous freedom in having clear, strong convictions that can only come from the absolute truth of the Bible. And even when we may attend a church where there are social programs, service opportunities, and solid teaching on Sunday mornings, it's not always enough to give us the knowledge and the tools we need to navigate our own spiritual growth with confidence.

The more we know and understand what's in the Bible, the more we will be able to live as we were truly created to live, confident of our identities and our beliefs so that we will love well and own our faith with new certainty. Knowing the Bible helps us navigate our complicated lives as we juggle calendars, families, relationships, and jobs. As women, we are often the main characters of all kinds of stories. Many of us are wives or mothers. We may be managers, employees, or entrepreneurs. Some carry the weight of growing up in a dysfunctional family, while others may be nursing broken hearts from relationships or circumstances gone awry. We also may find ourselves at times exhilarated by a victory or reveling in a hard-earned accomplishment. In our relationships and circumstances, we may wonder if we do and say the right things to be effective. Are we kind enough or assertive enough? Many of us question our purpose or our value in this world.

Conversely, have you spent any time with a woman who has seemingly been blessed with abundant confidence and clarity about why she was put on this earth? Where does that confidence come from? And how does she seem to bring light and energy to a room, lifting up people she talks to? Chances are great that she has internalized and personalized all that God has revealed to her in Scripture. It's that powerful. But that power comes with intentionality.

The Bible can be overwhelming and intimidating when we consider it as a lengthy, varied piece of literature, let alone when we accept its importance as a divinely-inspired spiritual guide, written over the span of 1500 years by many individuals. Because God is the author of the Bible, real freedom and conviction come from knowing His Word. Consider the following:

* ✷ The Bible is where God reveals Himself—His character, His purpose, His ways.

* ✷ The Bible is where we see ourselves accurately. Human nature in general as well as specific conviction for life change can be found by reading and knowing Scripture.

* ✷ The Bible gives us a world view based on absolute truth.

* ✷ The Bible provides cultural references that are practical in everyday relationships and conversations.

Psalm 119:151 says, "...*you are near, O Lord, and all your commandments are true.*" God wants relationship, and He has good things to teach us from His Word.

But where do we begin?

If we want to be effective learners, we need a plan. Knowing how the Bible was put together and what's in there will aid us in approaching it with less trepidation, so let's look at how the Bible is organized.

There are 66 books in the Bible, spanning 1500 years and multiple authors, all inspired by God to tell one story about Him. These books are divided into the Old Testament and the New Testament, and most Bibles have a table of contents in the beginning so you can find the book you're looking for. Here is an outline of the organization of the books of the Bible.

The Bible: God's Story

There are two parts of God's Word. The Old Testament is made up of 39 books. The New Testament is made up of 27 books. Each book has chapters, and each chapter has many verses. When you want to find something in the Bible, you can look up its "reference." The reference, *Genesis 1:1*, for example, means the book is Genesis, chapter 1, verse 1.

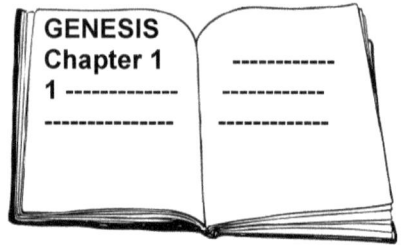

Genesis 1:1

The Old Testament

The Old Testament is the story of a promise, and every part of the Old Testament refers to this promise. Sometimes the promise is referred to as a covenant.

THE BOOKS OF THE LAW

The books of the law are the first five books of the Old Testament. They include the stories of the beginning of the world and the creation of the nation God called His own. God freed His nation from slavery, brought them through a raging sea, sent them food from the sky and water from the rocks. All He asked was that they obey His laws. Over and over again the people disobeyed. So God promised a way to make things right.

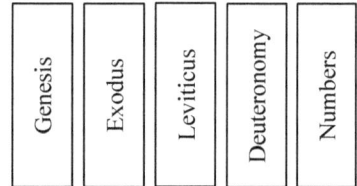

Genesis Exodus Leviticus Deuteronomy Numbers

THE BOOKS OF HISTORY

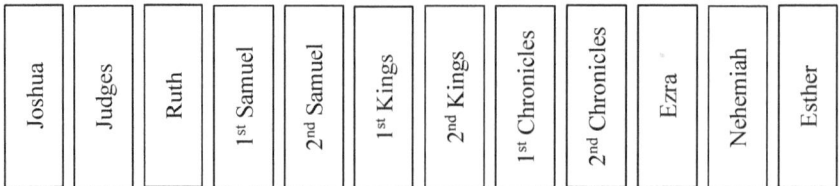

Joshua Judges Ruth 1st Samuel 2nd Samuel 1st Kings 2nd Kings 1st Chronicles 2nd Chronicles Ezra Nehemiah Esther

The books of history tell the story of God bringing His nation to a new homeland, helping them defeat their enemies, and allowing them to choose kings to rule over them. Sometimes people remembered God and His laws, but more often they did what they wanted. The nation had a civil war and both nations were carried away into captivity and exile by their enemies. Then the people had only God's promise that He would give them back their nation and would send the greatest king of all time.

THE BOOKS OF POETRY

These poetry books describe God's greatness and the beauty of His creation. They also contain advice about how to live a life that will please God.

Job | Psalms | Proverbs | Ecclesiastes | Song of Songs

MAJOR PROPHETS

Isaiah | Jeremiah | Lamentations | Ezekiel | Daniel

MINOR PROPHETS

Hosea | Joel | Amos | Obadiah | Jonah | Micah | Nahum | Habakkuk | Zephaniah | Haggai | Zechariah | Malachi

During the time of the books of history, God was speaking His messages of warning, punishment, and future redemption through messengers called prophets so the people would obey and live in the way God knew was best for them. Most prophets were sent during times of war and oppression. These messages also contained promises of restoration and a new king. Major prophets are called "major" because of the length of the books that bear their name; minor prophets are just shorter books—not less important.

The Old Testament spans the historical period roughly between 4000 B. C. and 430 B. C. The first 5 books of the Bible—Genesis, Exodus, Leviticus, Numbers, and Deuteronomy—are often referred to as the Torah. All of the Old Testament is the Jewish Bible and it has remained very much the same from the time Jesus would have read it as a young Jewish boy until what we read today. When we read the Old Testament, we are reading the same Bible Jesus read!

Other books in the Old Testament fall into just a few categories; there are books of poetry and wisdom, prophecy, and history. They are not arranged chronologically, however, so it takes time to recognize how the various accounts in one book fit into history with the others. Thankfully, there are many timelines available to help us with a frame of reference.

The New Testament

The New Testament records how God's promises from the Old Testament came true. Men who saw the promise come true wrote down exactly how it happened. Other men wrote about what that promise means to those who would follow Jesus.

THE GOSPELS

The Gospel writers tell us about the special birth of Jesus, God's Son. They describe the events of Jesus' life and how He loved to help people and teach them about His Father. They also tell us how Jesus made the words of the prophets come true when He died on the cross. The most exciting part of the Gospels is the last event. It tells us that Jesus came back to life and that He is waiting in heaven to come to Earth again.

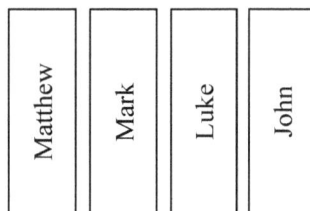

Matthew   Mark   Luke   John

HISTORY

Although Jesus' death may have felt like the end of the story and the end of the promise God had made, it was only the beginning. He rose from the dead and told His disciples to tell the good news to the whole world. The book of Acts recounts how people listened to the good news and believed in Jesus. Those Christians then began sharing the news with everyone in the world. The first missionaries!

Acts

LETTERS BY PAUL

LETTERS TO CHURCHES   INDIVIDUALS

Romans	1st Corinthians	2nd Corinthians	Galatians	Ephesians	Philippians	Colossians	1st Thessalonians	2nd Thessalonians	1st Timothy	2nd Timothy	Titus	Philemon

Paul was a man who had once tried to destroy Jesus' followers, but he became one of Christ's best-known servants after a dramatic encounter with God. He traveled to many countries, starting new churches wherever people listened and believed. When Paul left a group of Christians, he often wrote letter to them, explaining what they should believe and how they should behave. He also wrote letters to individuals.

GENERAL LETTERS

Hebrews	James	1st Peter	2nd Peter	1st John	2nd John	3rd John	Jude

Other followers of Jesus also wrote letters that gave the new churches the help they needed. These letters provided more information about Jesus as well as teachings on how to live out the Christian faith. Being a Christian wasn't easy in the early years after Jesus' resurrection, so these letters encouraged new believers.

PROPHECY

In the book of Revelation, one of Jesus' disciples records what God revealed to him regarding events in the future, when Jesus will come back to Earth demonstrating that He is the King of Kings!

Revelation

The New Testament starts with the life of Jesus. All the books of the New Testament either tell the story of his life, death, and resurrection, or mention Him and His teachings. These books cover the period of 6 B. C. to approximately 95 A. D. Matthew, Mark, Luke, and John are the first 4 books of the New Testament, and they simply recount the words Jesus said, His miracles, and the events surrounding His birth, life, death, and resurrection. Most of the rest of the books of the New Testament are letters written to those who lived in the time after Jesus' resurrection so that they could more fully understand the implications and applications of all Jesus did and taught.

Catholic Bibles have certain books in them that Protestant Bibles do not. They are *1 and 2 Esdras, Additions to Esther, 1 and 2 Macabees, Tobias, Judith, Wisdom, Sirach, Baruch, Epistle of Jeremiah, Susanna, Prayer of Azariah, Prayer of Manasseh, Bel and the Dragon, and Laodiceans.* They are all Old Testament period books and are referred to as the Apocrypha. There have never been any original Hebrew manuscripts discovered of these books, and certain denominations throughout the centuries have disagreed on whether these books are divinely inspired or merely educational and supplementary. During the middle ages these books fell out of use, and during the Reformation in the 16th century, when Martin Luther translated the Bible into German, he placed these books in a separate section. Later, when printing became more common, some publishers included them and some left them out.

All Bibles that you will find in English were translated from original documents and reliable copies, in Hebrew, Greek, or Aramaic, found in various parts of the world. The first English translation was done by John Wycliffe in 1382, fueled by his belief that everyone, not just priests and scholars, should be able to interact with God's Word.

In the 16th century, Martin Luther, famous for his outspoken criticism of the corruption of the Catholic Church at the time, translated the Bible into vernacular German so everyone could understand it. Around the same time, William Tyndale was working on an English Translation of the Bible from Hebrew and Greek texts.

King James I of England was in power in 1611 when an English translation of the Bible was printed and agreed upon by both Catholics and

Protestants. This translation is still widely read today and is named after him: The King James version of the Bible.

In recent centuries, there have been many translations in languages spoken and read worldwide. Each translation comes from the original languages and is either considered a word-for-word translation or an idea-for-idea translation. There are also paraphrased versions which are very accessible and easy to read, but not always appropriate for in-depth study.

In all of the translations over the years, there is a remarkable consistency in language and message, underscoring the trustworthiness of its divine Author—God Himself. Therefore, although not everything in the Bible may be specifically relevant to us in any given season or circumstance, all of it reveals something about God. That alone makes it worth reading. There is no other place to find such extensive descriptions of God so that we can truly know what He is like. In addition to that, we will find many practical applications for a variety of life situations. The Bible provides a reliable framework for us to construct a worldview, to navigate relationships, and to resist temptation. Jesus Himself used Scripture to withstand the devil's attacks when He was in the desert for 40 days after His baptism.

While each book of the Bible is unique in its purpose and scope, all Scripture reveals God and can change us if we let it. Then, as we study each book individually, we can also ask questions that are unique to that book. In our attempt to understand Scripture, we will get out of the experience what we put into it. Our best experiences will be when we come to God's Word expectantly, asking Him to reveal Himself and His timeless truth to us. We can also ask the Holy Spirit to show us specific ways that we can apply the lessons we're learning to our current circumstances.

Before we add any new knowledge to our brains, it's a good idea to identify what we already know. I like to think of learning like Velcro® in that it's only effective in holding things together if both parts are present. Every new piece of information we have will be stickier in our brains if we find a way to attach it to information that's already relevant and established in our minds.

Who are the characters you already know in Scripture? What are the themes and stories that are familiar to you from Sunday School, books you've read, or your own study? Connect as much of new information as possible to the Velcro® you already have in your brain. Studying the Bible and learning from it is just like anything else in life; we make an effort, we keep trying, and we celebrate the growth and new knowledge as success.

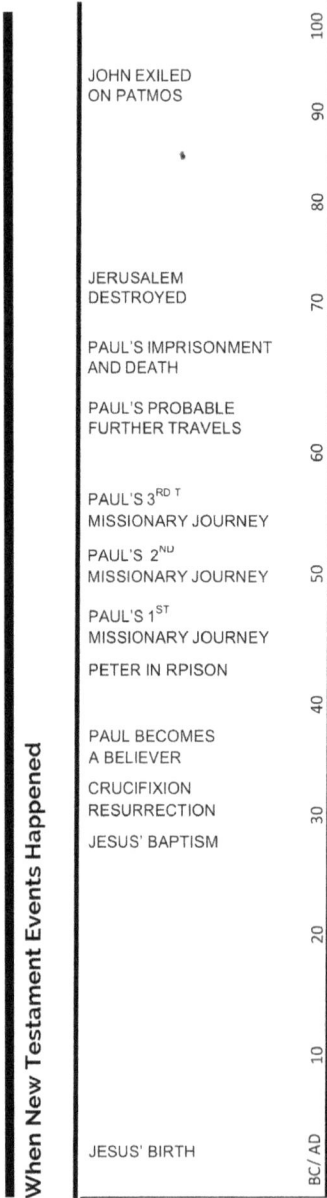

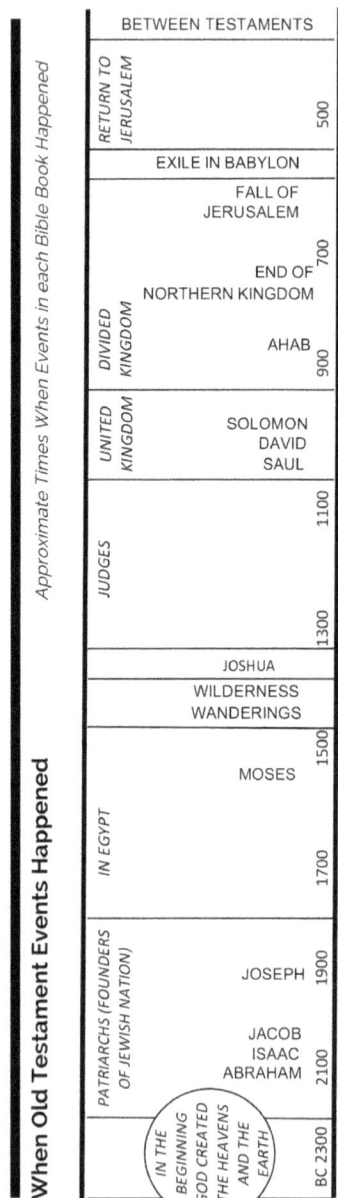

When New Testament Events Happened

Event	Approx. Date (BC/AD)
	100
JOHN EXILED ON PATMOS	90
	80
JERUSALEM DESTROYED	70
PAUL'S IMPRISONMENT AND DEATH	
PAUL'S PROBABLE FURTHER TRAVELS	
	60
PAUL'S 3RD T MISSIONARY JOURNEY	
PAUL'S 2ND MISSIONARY JOURNEY	
	50
PAUL'S 1ST MISSIONARY JOURNEY	
PETER IN RPISON	
	40
PAUL BECOMES A BELIEVER	
CRUCIFIXION RESURRECTION	30
JESUS' BAPTISM	
	20
	10
JESUS' BIRTH	BC/AD

When Old Testament Events Happened

Approximate Times When Events in each Bible Book Happened

Period	Event	Approx. Date (BC)
	BETWEEN TESTAMENTS	
RETURN TO JERUSALEM		500
	EXILE IN BABYLON	
	FALL OF JERUSALEM	
		700
DIVIDED KINGDOM	END OF NORTHERN KINGDOM	
	AHAB	900
UNITED KINGDOM	SOLOMON DAVID SAUL	
		1100
JUDGES		
		1300
	JOSHUA	
	WILDERNESS WANDERINGS	
IN EGYPT		1500
	MOSES	
		1700
PATRIARCHS (FOUNDERS OF JEWISH NATION)		
	JOSEPH	1900
	JACOB ISAAC ABRAHAM	2100
IN THE BEGINNING GOD CREATED THE HEAVENS AND THE EARTH		BC 2300

No woman can invite others to have access to everything she's learned or experienced in a lifetime, so we each need to open Scripture for ourselves and add to our knowledge piece by piece.

Here are basic timelines of some major biblical events in history:

In addition to knowing the facts, people, and events of the Bible, powerful learning comes from encountering God in the process of studying. It's impressive to hear an explanation of how hydrogen converts to helium to cause stars to emit energy and light in space, but there's an added dimension to the information when we lie on our backs in the grass to gaze into the black sky and watch stars twinkle. If you have the opportunity to look at space through the lens of a telescope, so much the better to experience stars up close and personally!

There are two levels of engaging with Scripture: one is the acquisition of facts and information, which is where we must begin, and the other is the interaction we have with God Himself. The latter encounter is when we open His Word to allow the Holy Spirit to be our teacher, convicting and transforming us in the process. The entire Bible tells God's story, reveals His character, and has value for us in our modern lives, so simply giving intellectual assent to the facts is only the beginning of the transformation process.

John Piper describes this well in his book, *Reading the Bible Supernaturally*:

> This is how God has designed the Scriptures to work for human transformation and for the glory of God: The Scriptures *reveal* God's glory. This glory, God willing, is *seen* by those who read the Bible. This seeing gives rise, by God's grace to *savoring* God above all things—treasuring him, hoping in him, feeling him as our greatest reward, tasting him as our all-satisfying good. And this savoring *transforms* our lives—freeing us from the slavery of selfishness and overflowing in love to others. This joy-sustained, God-exalting transformation of love is then *seen by others*, who, by God's grace, glorify God because of it. This movement rises and falls through history according to the faithfulness of Christ's people and the renewal of God's mercies.[2]

We engage our minds and depend on God to reveal His glory to our hearts. But what does all this have to do with stars?

Stars shine because their cores fuse hydrogen into helium. Stars orbit around the center of gravity in the galaxy. As followers of Christ, our cores and our centers of gravity must be based on truth. That truth can only be found in Scripture, but it's not just intellectual assent to facts and principles. It must also be engaging and transformational for it to emit light and heat into the crooked and depraved world in which we live.

The *kosmos* (universe, sky) in which we're to shine like stars, is vast and dark and cold. Just like stars shine in the dark of the universe, we can shine in a crooked and perverse world by "holding firmly to the word of life." We can cling to what's true and be free from the bondage of lies. We can live out our convictions with boldness and love, out of a transformed life because we've encountered the glory of God in His Word. And to encounter Him is to more fully savor Him. That's what changes us and lets us shine. And this universe needs the light we bring. When we see it for all its crookedness and depravity and darkness, the light of Christ that we bring to it is stark in contrast. This is why it's so important that we shine.

Questions for Discussion or Application:

+ What questions or trepidation do you have concerning the Bible?

+ In what areas of life do you wish you were more familiar with what the Bible says?

+ Where would you look in the Bible for information about wisdom? Jesus' life, death, and resurrection? How to love people well? Witchcraft or occult practices?

Chapter 2

Shine

Before there were advanced technological means of navigation, sailors used to find their way on the seas by using the stars. And why did they use stars? Because they shone. And even though the constellations weren't always in the same place in the sky in every season, it wasn't the stars that had moved; the Earth had. Earth rotates and orbits around the sun—a star.

In astronomy, a star is a massive, luminous ball of plasma. The ball of plasma has a dense core of hydrogen that burns and radiates energy through nuclear fusion. This gives it heat and it's why we see a star as light.

When it comes to people, we've heard celebrities referred to as stars. Movie stars. TV stars. Rock stars. We call them stars because they seem to shine more brightly than the rest of us. There's something different about them. Maybe they're more talented than the average person. Maybe they're better looking. Or they might just have more money. We give them stars on Hollywood Boulevard and we call them stars because they shine.

But the way God calls us to shine is something different.

Living our lives for God enables us to shine like stars among a dark and crooked generation that doesn't acknowledge Him. As we meet other Christians doing the same, we will find that we have many characteristics in common with one another. Here's a partial list of what the Bible says is true about us:

* We were uniquely and wonderfully made by God. (Psalm 139:13-16)

* We have all fallen short of God's perfect standard and can do nothing to earn His love and acceptance. (Romans 3:23)

* We were chosen, forgiven, and brought into God's eternal family through the death and resurrection of Jesus. (Ephesians 1:4-12)

* We have been set apart to live lives that reflect God's love and glory to the world. (1 Peter 2:9)

* We are more than improved versions of our former selves; we are NEW creations. (2 Corinthians 5:17)

* We have the Holy Spirit in us to guide, convict, and transform us to be more like Jesus. (Ephesians 1:13-14; John 14:15-17, 16:7-15)

The first two statements are true from the time of conception for everyone. The rest of the statements are true from the moment we respond to Jesus' invitation to trust Him. Once we've committed to follow Him with our whole hearts for our whole lives, our identities are eternally changed!

Then attitude and behavior changes begin to occur as we learn, grow, and are challenged by Scripture, the Holy Spirit, and those around us. Certain characteristics appear in others and in us as we cultivate our relationship with God, and we begin to look and act the way God designed us to. We will *listen* to God and others. We will *serve* others and *submit* to God. We will be *loving* and *obedient*. We will be getting truth from God's Word and confessing our sin as we try to stay connected to Him. These are all ongoing processes and activities that ebb and flow in our lives over time, but they are what differentiates us from those in the world who have not chosen to follow Jesus.

If we look at the shape of a star as we see it in art and decorating schemes, we notice five points. These points for us can represent spiritual disciplines that will help us maintain our consistency in pursuing our relationship with God. Each point reminds us of actions we can take or attitudes and areas of life where we can evaluate our progress in our Christian walk.

I have found that this image is helpful in describing some of the characteristics that will define us as Jesus-followers within the context of stars:

LISTEN

SUBMIT   SERVE

OBEY   LOVE

Let's take a look at why each of these elements is important to help us shine.

Listen

Listen is at the top of the star as it indicates the position of prominence that it plays in our relationship with God and with others. King Solomon gave good direction as to why listening in prayer is important when he wrote, *"Do not be quick with your mouth, do not be hasty in your heart to utter anything before God. God is in heaven and you are on earth, so let your words be few"* (Ecclesiastes 5:2).

Dick Eastman, in his book *The Hour That Changes the World*, wrote, "to listen in prayer is to mentally absorb divine instructions from God concerning specific matters for that day."[1] It is imperative that we distinguish our Father's voice from all the other voices that vie for our attention, so practicing the art of listening is an integral part of our relationship with God. So much of our devotional life may be about our own efforts—*our* Bible study, *our* intercession for friends, *our* list of requests. Intentionally listening places the focus back on God and His divine direction for our lives.

In that time of silence, when we invite God to speak, He may give words of encouragement, specific direction, revelation of sin, or words of affirmation and love. These messages may be for our own benefit or for us to pass along to others. Faith comes into play when we decide whether or not to move according to what we hear.

One of the best attitudes we can adopt is that of young Samuel when he heard God's voice for the first time when under Eli's tutelage: *"Speak, for your servant is listening."* What God says to us is far more important than anything we have to say to Him. His voice informs ours and is the voice of perfect love and truth.

It's important that we exercise our listening muscles with God, and it may help to think about how this works when we communicate with other people. Conversation is a 2-way experience; few people would argue with that. In theory. However, we often spend more time talking or forming our responses to our partner's piece of the conversation rather than actively listening for meaning and understanding. Susan Scott, author and consultant to CEOs around the world, helps professionals have conversations with peers, customers, and employees to maximize time and energy. Her book *Fierce Conversations* has dramatically changed the way I communicate with others both professionally and personally, and I quote her readily and frequently when I speak for groups. The most important elements of a conversation, she points out, are silence and listening to what others have to say. She uses the analogy of a beach ball with sections of color, explaining that in any organization, each person or section is one of those colors and sees the entire group with a filter of their particular hue.[2] If I am in sales, I see the whole business in terms of sales, and don't see expanding another "color" as a priority. If I'm engaged with the children's ministry of my church, I will think of the whole church in terms of my area of need and activity, not realizing how other "colors" may be affected.

We only get to the whole truth of any situation by listening to others and hearing their perspective. And we can only do that well if we have already listened to what God has to say to us. If we are going to shine like stars in a world that's ruled by darkness, we would do well to listen to God first, then to those He has placed in our sphere of influence. Then we will know how to pray for them and to speak to areas of their lives that God can illuminate. How can we *"be prepared to give an answer to everyone who asks us to give the reason for the hope that you have"* (1 Peter 3:15) if we don't listen to the questions?

Serve

Going around our star clockwise, we come to the word "Serve." Jesus said that whatever we do for "the least of these" we have done for Him. This means the people in our lives who need help. Getting our hands dirty and working for the good of others is a huge piece of the Christian life that lets the love of God shine brightly in the world. When we serve others in whatever capacity God calls us to, it's harder to focus on ourselves, and that's a good thing! Ephesians 6:7 exhorts us to *"Serve wholeheartedly, as if you were serving the Lord, not men, because you know that the Lord will reward everyone for whatever good he does whether he is slave or free."* The New Testament only uses this Greek word "wholeheartedly" twice. It means to do something sincerely, with eagerness and enthusiasm. It means that we do it with a happy heart and that we do it without expecting any thanks or reciprocal service from the one we serve because God is the one who will reward us. Paul's use of the word here is in the context of slaves serving their masters well—with all their hearts and good will. This is easier and more natural for some than others, but it's part of the process for all of us. When we are watching for God's activity and listening for His Spirit to prompt us to serve someone else, we have to be willing to lay aside our needs and agendas to comply. One way we shine as stars is to serve people without expecting anything in return. Again, we listen for God and depend on his Spirit to empower us; then we move in response.

What does it look like? Serving takes as many forms as there are personalities and opportunities, which is why it's so important to do spiritual gifts inventories that reveal clues about how God has wired us. It may be cooking food for a local homeless shelter, organizing shelves at the food bank, helping someone move, cleaning a house, teaching Sunday School, serving medically, or setting up chairs for a meeting. If you've been served by someone who simply showed up and did something for you that blessed you, you know the profound impact service can have. We serve out of strength, with energy that comes from knowing the God who saved us and made us. And when there is no strength in us to serve, we admit our weakness to God and He replaces our weakness with His strength to do what He asks us to do. A visible and powerful way we shine as stars is to serve people without expecting anything in return.

Submit

Submission is a fun word, isn't it? Well, if service is about the physicality of our spiritual journey, then submission is about the attitude of our hearts. One without the other is not Christian. James 4:7 sums up what we need to remember about this aspect of shining: *"Submit yourselves to God."* It doesn't get any simpler than that, does it? Submission is about choosing not to strong arm our own plans, but to allow God to dictate the situations in our lives. The second half of James 4:7 reveals something about the concept of submission: *"Submit yourselves, then, to God. Resist the devil, and he will flee from you."* The verse that follows this one delivers a cause-effect relationship: *"Come near to God and He will come near to you."* When we choose to submit to God's authority and sovereignty, Satan loses. When we insist on our own rights, Satan wins. When we choose submission, Satan flees. But submitting can only happen successfully when we come near to God. Far from Him, there is no power or desire to submit.

I once heard a story about a toddler who refused to listen to his mother when she told him repeatedly to sit down. Finally, perhaps realizing that this was an argument he could not win, the boy sat down, saying to his mother, "I'm sitting on the outside, but I'm still standing up on the inside." This is the opposite of submission to God! He wants our hearts to submit as well as our bodies. Submission means acknowledging that God's way is best. Am I fighting for my way? Insisting on my rights? Do I persist in areas of disobedience? Or do I acknowledge God's power and goodness in my life so that I lay down any sense of entitlement I may be carrying to accept what He has for me.

Another image that may be helpful is to think of royalty like the British Queen. There is strict protocol concerning an encounter with the royal family; men are expected to bow and women are expected to curtsey. Terms used to address each member of the royal family are also dictated in order to show the respect due the sovereign of the nation. From a distance, there isn't much protocol necessary, but when we approach the sovereign, we more fully recognize his or her standing as royalty, and our actions and attitudes reflect that. For example, once when visiting Berlin, our group was on the street when a motorcade of Norwegian royalty drove by. There was no need for us to bow or curtsey, but if we had attended a social occasion and met them in person, things might have been different. Even in that case, since I'm not a Norwegian citizen, I'm not obligated to submit. Scripture tells us that we are not citizens of this world but of God's kingdom. Therefore, God is our king—our sovereign king—and submission to the king is expected. Moreover, ours is an all-powerful, benevolent king who only has our best interest in mind.

Submission is a conscious act of the will, a choice to follow and obey a voice other than our own. Other words that describe this concept are *yield* or *surrender*. We choose to let God guide, speak, and direct us. A bowing of the heart, if you will. In that posture, God will meet us, speak to us, and change us.

After Charlie was born, Tony and I actively pursued a second pregnancy. We wanted children, plural. But none came. I was disappointed; I was resentful of my friends' pregnancies; I was especially bitter about women who complained to me about the fact that they were "pregnant again! Can you believe it?" For years I cried and pleaded with God. But I didn't submit. I didn't acknowledge that God's plan for us was, in fact, perfect. I wasn't satisfied in the blessings He had given me; I hadn't recognized His goodness. Instead, I wallowed in self-pity and shook my fist at God when someone else got the blessing I was denied.

Years later, I can say that God knew what He was doing by giving us only one. I joke and say that we have gotten our money's worth out of the one kid God gave us! But I can also say that I have learned what it means to say, over and over again, that God is in control. He is God; I am not. I accept what He gives me because He alone is my portion. And I am satisfied.

Love and Obey

The reason these two points of the star are grouped together is because love for God and obedience to Him are inextricably linked. Look at this verse from 2nd John 1:6: "*And this is love: that we walk in obedience to his commands. As you have heard me say from the beginning, his command is that you walk in love.*" Walking in love means walking in obedience. You can walk a lot longer than you can run, can't you? The Christian journey is more like a marathon than a sprint, and learning to walk in love and obedience takes time and practice. Training, if you will. But as we learn to love Him and receive His love for us, obedience becomes easier and more natural because loving God reveals His power and sovereignty so we can trust Him with our lives, taking risks to do what He calls us to do.

Look at Romans 6:15-18:

> *Well then, since God's grace has set us free from the law, does that mean we can go on sinning? Of course not! Don't you realize that you become the slave of whatever you choose to obey? You can be a slave to sin, which leads to death, or you can choose to obey God, which leads to righteous living. Thank God! Once you were slaves of sin, but now you wholeheartedly obey this teaching we have given you. Now you are free from your slavery to sin, and you have become slaves to righteous living.* (NLT)

These verses are a great picture of the combination of God's work and our participation in the transformation process. God has set us free from sin by the death and resurrection of Jesus. All the power that raised Christ from the dead is available to us through that relationship. Then we choose to obey because we understand love. How do we achieve that level of comfort with obedience? The Roman Christians made Paul so proud because they used to be slaves to sin, but then they obeyed the teaching they received. Wholeheartedly. There's that word again. To serve and obey wholeheartedly requires a conscious decision for us to be fully involved in the process. There's a Stephen Curtis Chapman song from several years ago called *Whatever.* The chorus says, "Whatever. Whatever you say. Whatever. I will obey.

Whatever. Lord, have your way. For you are my God...whatever." Those are words of a heart that understands God's goodness and is willing to obey His will, no matter what. Easy or hard. Now or later. Whatever.

If we stand with our feet apart and arms out to our sides, we can become the shape of a star to help us remember these points in our lives. We *listen* with our ears, which are on our heads; we *serve* with our dominant hand to remember that we should do it with strength and intention, not out of some halfhearted, leftover energy; we *submit* with our non-dominant hand to remind us that God is our strength and that surrender to Him is good for our character; and we *obey* and *love* by going with our feet where God leads us, walking into the good works He's created us for.

So these five points of the star can help us gauge our growth as we grow in our relationship with God and with each other, but the way that looks in each of our lives will be very different, depending on our personalities, our circumstances, and our calling. There are things that are true of all of God's children, and there are things that are uniquely true about you. Everyone has spiritual gifts and was created in God's image; each of us uses those gifts and bears that image in a way that God designed specifically for us.

Shining Uniquely

You may have heard of a personality test called the Myers-Briggs Type Indicator®. It's a classic assessment used to determine strengths and preferences that many believe are in our DNA to be revealed over time as we mature. The test attempts to make sense of the theory of psychological types described by Karl Jung, Swiss psychoanalyst practicing in the early 20th century, so that we can more easily recognize and understand our preferences and behaviors in everyday life.

The four areas of personality that this assessment helps to clarify are 1) how you get your energy, 2) how you take in information, 3) how you make decisions, and 4) how you prefer your world to be organized. Your official Myers-Briggs Personality Type is then expressed as a code with four letters, each indicating your preference for each of the areas of life mentioned.[3]

This is just one of many examples of ways that psychology gives labels to the unique traits each of us possesses as human beings. Donald O. Clifton, Ph.D., Tom Rath, and a team of scientists at Gallup developed a series of useful diagnostic tools for professionals in the early 2000s called Strengthsfinder®. This book and assessment help identify a person's unique combination of 34 strengths so that everyone can spend more time doing what they love and do best.[4]

Spiritual gifts inventories tell us in which ways the Holy Spirit has gifted us to serve the body of Christ and grow the kingdom for God's glory.

These and many other tools and studies tell us that, like stars, people are unique and wonderful in their special abilities and tendencies. This is why the Bible describes us as being "fearfully and wonderfully made". (Psalm 139:14). And since each of us is unique not only in our strengths and personalities, but also in our experiences, temperaments, skills, and environment, we will all shine as stars in the place and way that God intended for us before He created the universe! The best way for each of us to shine is to know who we are and whose we are; then we can, as my friend and Myers-Briggs expert Jessica Butts says, "be unapologetically who we are!" [5]

My Myers-Briggs Type, for example, is **ESTJ**. Extrovert, Sensing, Thinking, Judging. This type is nicknamed "the Guardian." I like being around people—I get energy from it. I like systems and information and routine to a certain extent. I live and make decisions in my head, logically, not with my heart. I'm not good at sensing the vibe of a room, and I'm not naturally empathetic, nor a good listener. I also have a hard time identifying and articulating (and sometimes controlling) my emotions. When I'm hurt or stressed, I become very emotional and withdrawn. My buttons get pushed when things don't go according to plan or when someone says things that threaten or hurt me. Words are very powerful to me.

My spiritual gifts are teaching, prophecy and exhortation. I love, love, love reading the Bible and teaching it to others. I love encouraging Christian women in the truth of Scripture as it pertains to their everyday lives. I can often tell you exactly what Scripture passage reveals the truth of the situation you're in and I'll help you devise a plan to get to your goals.

I have found great satisfaction and success in things like being a high school teacher, teaching Bible studies, being a speaker in professional settings, being president of organizations, networking, and group activities. I don't feel guilty about not signing up to hold babies in the nursery or being a member of a prayer group or anything that works diligently behind the scenes setting up or making crafts. Knowing how God has wired me gives me the freedom to say yes *and* to say no. I appreciate people who do those things, but I'm not one of them. And the teams and the babies don't want me there, either, I promise. I'm 51 years old and I know what makes my heart sing and what breaks it. I purposely put systems in place to help me avoid my weaknesses and develop my strengths.

Now, if someone wrecks my systems or says things that hurt me, my worst self emerges. When the Holy Spirit is fueling my gifts and my activities, I shine and show the world what Jesus looks like. And I can say without a trace of bragging, "Look what God is doing through me! I was BORN for this!" But... When the Holy Spirit is NOT fueling my gifts and activities, I'm mean, petty, emotionally out of control, withdrawn, and generally unpleasant. My gifts turn into judgmental finger-wagging, and the effects are not good for relationships.

Both these things are true: I'm profoundly wicked and I'm wildly loved. We all live in that universal theological tension, but we also live in our own unique tension. My hope for you would be that you discover your strengths and gifts so that you can have an accurate assessment of yourself. Instead of feeling defeated or inferior when we see a weakness in ourselves, we can remember how God made us uniquely and what He wants us to be. This is freedom! It's an opportunity to let God shine through us as He reveals the best of what He's put in us.

The Bible Tells Me So

So how can we know who God created us to be? Where do we look to discover what's true about all Christians? The best place to see what God says about His children is in Scripture. The verses at the beginning of this chapter are a start, but both the Old and New Testaments are replete with descriptions of God's creation of, love for, and redemption of His chosen people. The Old Testament tells the story of God's choice of Israel as His people, how He felt about them, and what He required of them to experience His blessings. There are hundreds and hundreds of pages over thousands of years that reveal inconsistent emotions and universal human nature juxtaposed with a perfect, consistent, powerful Creator. When we read about who God is and who we are—just like the millions of people in the Bible—we can take what life throws at us more easily and with equanimity, knowing that our experience is not greater than God's love or His power to reach and console us. Through the Old Testament we learn that God is powerful and loves His imperfect and rebellious creation.

The New Testament depicts the manifestation of God's plan to redeem His beloved children from the sin that keeps them from enjoying relationship with Him both now and for eternity. In the perfect time, God sent Jesus—perfect in his human obedience and full of divine nature—to settle the debt we owed for offending the Creator and King of the universe. The gospels are four accounts of the life, ministry, death, and resurrection of Jesus. In the book of Acts we see the formation of the 1st century church, including miraculous acts of the Holy Spirit as He inhabited people in a new way. The letters Paul and others wrote in the early days of Christianity give us glimpses into the struggles that our faith predecessors engaged in and reminds us of why the struggles matter and who is ultimately powerful enough to guide and comfort us.

In both sections of Scripture, God tells His people who He is and who they are. That's where we start. Then, by spending time with God, reading His truth and listening to His Spirit, we begin to understand who we are as unique and beloved individuals. With the parameters of unchanging biblical principles and the examples of those who have gone before us, we can then listen to the promptings of the Spirit to lead us on our particular path, knowing that a loving and powerful God has His hand on us.

Stars shine because of the nuclear fusion happening in their cores. Christians shine because at our core, we know who we are and whose we are.

This gives us confidence to speak boldly, with conviction, and in love. The light we shine into the world is from the Holy Spirit in us, igniting us to be everything that our loving and artistic Creator designed us to be. We shine as we *listen* to God, *serve* others as He prompts us, *submit* to His sovereign will in our lives and in the world, and as we walk in the characteristic *love* and *obedience* that are hallmarks of those who belong to Jesus.

But this process doesn't happen effortlessly or overnight. The transformation of our lives into shining stars for His glory is a combination of God doing what only He can do and then our response to that miracle. The five points of this star image are examples of our response to God's activity in our lives, but just like a star, we don't end up the way we begin.

Questions for Discussion or Application:

+ In which point of the star do you find easiest to participate? Which is most challenging? Why?

+ What are your spiritual gifts? Where have you seen evidence of your gifts in your community of faith? How are you using them?

Chapter 3

Transformation

Stars are born when there is a change in surroundings. They're born in a cloud of dust, debris, and darkness, when the gas and debris are disturbed by something. This might be a nearby explosion, another star passing by, or a galaxy collision, which changes the atmosphere. Dust and debris spin, causing friction, which produces heat. The dust then compresses and nuclear fusion begins. Hydrogen turns into helium, producing heat and light.

And even though the birth of all stars looks similar, over the course of their lifetimes, stars vary in brightness, size, and temperature. More massive stars have a shorter life as their mass causes them to burn through the elements more quickly. Stars with low mass burn slowly and have long lives. Our Sun is a medium star and it will swell up in a billion or more years to become a red giant, then a white dwarf, eventually burning itself out.

When stars use up all the hydrogen in their cores, so that it stops becoming helium, the core will start fusing other elements, like carbon, neon, and finally, iron. Over time, the star's temperature increases and it becomes slightly larger. Low mass stars like red dwarfs slowly collapse and cool over the course of many years. Or they may start to fuse the outer layers of the star and become bigger and bigger, burning off some of those outer layers in bursts, until all the hydrogen is used and the star cools to become a white dwarf. All stars eventually either become white dwarfs, which are smaller stars with more density, or neutron stars, which are even more dense because atoms have been crushed. They also may become black holes, the densest finale of them all. This is an object so dense that not even light can escape to be seen.

Spiritual Birth

When we first encountered Christ, it may have been because there was a lot of heat or friction in our lives and we were desperate for something or someone bigger than ourselves. It may have been because someone came into our lives and looked, acted, or spoke in such a way that it caused us to become curious and pursue something spiritually. Even if we were raised in a community of faith with parents and siblings who always spoke about Jesus and followed Him, there was a season or a moment when we made that journey our own. We accepted Jesus for who He said He was: Savior of our souls and Lord of our lives. This is when spiritual fusion began. And when that spiritual journey begins, we are often still living among the dust and debris of our former lives.

Then, as we learn more about how much God loves us, we continually listen, submit, and obey. That's when we begin to see change in our lives. We are transformed. Our core—the center of our lives—is fueled by the Holy Spirit, and we shine in the darkness around us as God's Spirit does the transformational work on the inside. And ultimately, as we follow Christ for our whole lives, His Spirit will continue to burn within us so that whatever shape our final days may take, there will still be light shining around us so others can see Jesus in us. No spiritual black holes! We want to keep shining!

But just like stars go through their transformations over the course of many years, it's a lifelong process for us to learn how to really shine.

Remember the verses from Philippians that talk about stars?

> *Do everything without grumbling or arguing, so that you may become blameless and pure, "children of God without fault in a warped and crooked generation." Then you will shine among them like stars in the sky as you hold firmly to the word of life...*
>
> (Philippians 2:14-16)

Why does Paul exhort the Philippians to act this way? To Do EVERY-THING without grumbling or arguing? So that they will *"become blameless and pure, children of God without fault in a warped and crooked generation."* BECOME implies a process. And the end result is purity—no blame, no fault. We will be perfect. In heaven. Until then we are all in process, getting closer to the goal.

While we're being transformed we can be lights that shine in the darkness. We can be a kind of straight line among that which is crooked. **Crooked**: *not aligned properly, curved or bent, illegal or dishonest.* Anybody see that in the world around them? It's hard to miss that part of the world no matter where we spend our time. That's the darkness of the world's perspective. Live for immediate pleasure and gain. Do what's good for yourself. Money and fame matter most. It's imperative that we shine in a dark world! Now more than ever, because now is all we have!

And while we will depend on God and make every effort to shine and not live like the rest of the world, we aren't to feel proud because we've achieved some level of higher morality. Paul reminds us in 1 Corinthians 6:9-11:

> *Do you not know that the wicked will not inherit the kingdom of God? Do not be deceived: Neither the sexually immoral nor idolaters nor adulterers nor male prostitutes nor homosexual offenders nor thieves nor the greedy nor drunkards nor slanderers nor swindlers will inherit the kingdom of God. And that is what some of you were. But you were washed, you were sanctified, you were justified in the name of the Lord Jesus Christ and by the Spirit of God.*

We were part of that crooked and depraved world; then we encountered the grace and love of Jesus. We *"were washed, sanctified, justified in the name of the Lord Jesus Christ and by the Spirit of God!"* God did the work to make the transformation possible; it is up to us to live up to the gift He's given us. So we can shine like stars. Pure. Luminescent. Bright. Clear. Jesus is the "word of life" Paul exhorts us to cling to. He alone makes it possible for us to shine, and He's the one the rest of the world needs to see in us.

Participating in that process is called sanctification—becoming more and more who we were created to be. More and more like Jesus. Look at 2 Corinthians 3:18:

> *We, who with unveiled faces all reflect the Lord's glory, are being transformed into His likeness with ever-increasing glory, which comes from the Lord, who is the Spirit.*

This is supposed to be our trajectory: growing more and more like Jesus. And where does that come from? *"... from the Lord, who is the Spirit."* The Holy Spirit is the source of our transformation. He alone brings fruit into our lives (Galatians 5), convicts us of sin (John 16), and intercedes for us in prayer when our hearts are heavy or our circumstances are unclear (Romans 8).

In the section before 2 Corinthians 3:18, Paul describes Moses and his return from special times meeting with God. After those encounters with God, Moses had to cover his face with a veil for two reasons. First, the effect of God's glory on Moses' face was just too much for the people. It caused as much fear as adoration and it was overwhelming. Second, if Moses didn't cover his face, the people would see the effect of God's glory fade. That fading glory would have been discouraging for the Hebrews. But that was only what the law did in lives apart from Jesus: it made us try harder and harder to win God's approval and achieve perfection. But the law doesn't give life. Jesus does. So Moses covered his face.

We, as those who love and follow Jesus, have what this verse calls "unveiled faces." We are called to live our faith out openly for everyone to see who we are and whose we are. And this open identity that's revealed is ever-changing with increasing glory—not diminishing glory like Moses' face—as the Spirit within us changes us to be more and more like Jesus.

This doesn't mean that we will effortlessly become holy and that we are passive in the transformation process. While we do trust the Holy Spirit to do in us what only He can do, we also participate, doing what God calls us to do. God has done His part in sending Jesus to die in our place so we can come into God's Presence and have relationship with Him now and forever. He has given us His Holy Spirit as a counselor and guide, and we have His power. We are forgiven, redeemed, and loved. There is nothing standing in the way of us becoming more and more like Jesus except us. We get in our own way a lot of times.

So what might this look like—this transformation process? How does it work to live the daily balance between God's part and our part?

We acknowledge and are grateful for the fact that God has saved us! We are loved, forgiven, redeemed, and nothing can change that. That's God's part. We learn this and are reminded of it every time we read Scripture, and it becomes our fuel and our motivation for doing what we do in response.

Then we go back to our star. We *listen, serve, submit, love,* and *obey* in response to what God has already done in us. This star and the principles attached to each point can help us participate wholeheartedly in the process to experience more of God and be more effective for His kingdom. That's how the transformation process happens.

Just like a star.

And just like a star, we don't start out the way we end up. Stars go through a sort of transformation process over the course of their lifetimes, just like we do.

Like stars, we all shine differently and appear differently to others. Some will burn brightly and many will experience the impact their lives make. Some will burn slowly and steadily all their lives, gently leading others to see what God is like. We are created uniquely and were born with different gifts, talents, interests and experiences, and God can use all of it to reveal Himself to others through us.

This is why it's so important to know how God made us. What are your spiritual gifts? What are you really good at? What kind of people do you attract? What personality type do you have? What makes your heart sing? Lean into those things so you can shine like God created you to shine!

The way we do these things and the way we shine will vary depending on our personalities, gifts, and circumstances, but we all belong to God's family and have been washed, sanctified, and justified. That's what makes us shine, regardless of our specific surroundings.

Look at the way Paul describes this partnership between God's provision for us and our participation in the transformation of our souls:

> *Therefore, there is now no condemnation for those who are in Christ Jesus, because through Christ Jesus the law of the Spirit who gives life has set you free from the law of sin and death. For what the law was power-less to do because it was weakened by the flesh, God did by sending his*

own Son in the likeness of sinful flesh to be a sin offering. And so he condemned sin in the flesh, in order that the righteous requirement of the law might be fully met in us, who do not live according to the flesh but according to the Spirit.

Those who live according to the flesh have their minds set on what the flesh desires; but those who live in accordance with the Spirit have their minds set on what the Spirit desires. The mind governed by the flesh is death, but the mind governed by the Spirit is life and peace. The mind governed by the flesh is hostile to God; it does not submit to God's law, nor can it do so. Those who are in the realm of the flesh cannot please God.

You, however, are not in the realm of the flesh but are in the realm of the Spirit, if indeed the Spirit of God lives in you. And if anyone does not have the Spirit of Christ, they do not belong to Christ. But if Christ is in you, then even though your body is subject to death because of sin, the Spirit gives life because of righteousness. And if the Spirit of him who raised Jesus from the dead is living in you, he who raised Christ from the dead will also give life to your mortal bodies because of his Spirit who lives in you.

Therefore, brothers and sisters, we have an obligation—but it is not to the flesh, to live according to it. For if you live according to the flesh, you will die; but if by the Spirit you put to death the misdeeds of the body, you will live.

For those who are led by the Spirit of God are the children of God. The Spirit you received does not make you slaves, so that you live in fear again; rather, the Spirit you received brought about your adoption to sonship. And by him we cry, "Abba, Father." The Spirit himself testifies with our spirit that we are God's children. Now if we are children, then we are heirs—heirs of God and co-heirs with Christ, if indeed we share in his sufferings in order that we may also share in his glory.

(Romans 8:1-17)

Notice the verses that point out what God has done for us to grow into ever-increasing glory:

God set you free from sin and death. (8:2)
God sent His son as a sin offering for us. (8:3)

The Holy Spirit gives life because of
(Christ's) righteousness. (8:10)
The Holy Spirit made us sons and daughters of God. (8:16)
God made us co-heirs with Christ. (8:17)

Intermingled with these doctrinal truths are our natural and heartfelt responses:

We live according to the Spirit. (8:4)
We set our minds on what God wants. (8:5)
We put to death sinful behavior. (8:13)

Ultimately, all our responses can be summed up by saying *"we have an obligation"* to live according to the ways of God as He reveals Himself and His ways to us. Once we have been brought to life from death, and freed from being slaves to sin, what other response is there? And the ongoing collaboration between God's supernatural work through the Holy Spirit and our response in choosing obedience will result in ever-increasing glory as we shine brightly like stars!

Here's an example of a beautiful transformation I've watched over the past decade or so. My niece Mary Kay came to live with us during a rather tumultuous time in her life. She came to Seattle from St. Louis when she was 18 and had burned some bridges with family there, so we were a logical landing place for her. In retrospect, I can also see that it was divinely orchestrated. There were conflicts and misunderstandings among us. We established a sort of "don't ask; don't tell" policy for nights she didn't come home at all. There were trips to the hospital for appendicitis and concussions. Broken car doors, many tears, and "true feelings" shared at the dinner table. It was the best of times; it was the worst of times.

After almost three years of living with us, after our traditional heart-shaped meatloaf family dinner on Valentine's Day, Mary Kay and I had a profound conversation that changed her eternal destination. She came to a realization that loving God was a two-way relationship that started with accepting Jesus' gift of forgiveness in her life, and we prayed together on our couch for her to commit her life to Jesus.

Months later, I made a three-day road trip with Mary Kay to move her back to St. Louis, and we had ample time to chat about her new faith. I remember like it was yesterday the question she asked as we alternated choosing music on the radio somewhere in Montana: Now that I'm a Christian do I have to stop listening to Usher?

She wanted and expected a list of rules and parameters to live her new life, and I was so glad to explain to her that having a relationship with Jesus was much, much more than that! I told her that no one could tell her the exact timeline or method for the Holy Spirit's transformation in her life except the Holy Spirit Himself, and that if she focused on learning about God and loving Him, He would do the transformation work in her over time.

Over the next few years I watched Mary Kay learn and grow and change to look more and more like the amazing woman God created her to be. Over time, she not only learned to read and understand the Bible on her own, but she also enrolled in seminary and earned two Masters Degrees! She's discovered her gifts and the people God has called her to love, and she is in the process of starting a high school for a unique and marginalized population of teens that will help them obtain diplomas and discover God's love for them. She will be the first to tell people that she has "room to grow in the way that she loves people," but she has also been the most dramatic example of that growth than just about anyone I've ever met. And she is very intentional about the music she listens to, but that's because God is directing it!

Her transformation is still in process, as is mine. And yours. It takes a lifetime for God to make us fully who we were created to be.

We're meant to be out and about in this world, shining like stars in a crooked and depraved generation, orbiting among the darkness, dust and debris. But that orbit isn't random; God's Spirit leads us and tethers us to Him as we move and live in the world. And if we're mindful of our center of gravity, we can be sure that our orbit doesn't take us too far from where we're supposed to be.

Questions for Discussion or Application:

+ What have you learned about your personality and/or spiritual gifts that you can apply to how you participate in the transformation process?

+ How have you experienced the balance between God's role and yours in your spiritual transformation?

+ How have you noticed the difference between living according to the flesh and living according to the Spirit?

Chapter 4

Orbit

Many of us learned in science class that the earth and all the other planets orbit around the sun. That's true. And although it may not be obvious from Earth, stars like our Sun orbit as well. It's not in a perfect circular motion like diagrams we may see in science books, but they don't usually orbit randomly, either. They may be in a binary star system, in which two stars orbit around a common center of mass, gravitationally bound to each other, or they might be part of larger group of stars that orbit around the center of the galaxy.[1]

They may also be like the Sun in our own solar system, orbiting individually around the center of the galaxy. What they all have in common is the fact that their gravitational center is something strong and dense at the center of the galaxy. Stars don't all move in the same way, but they are all drawn into some sort of orbit by gravity; something is pulling them at all times, and their path through the sky is connected to that gravitational pull until the star dies or until it collides with something else in space.

As Christians, we should also be intentional about and aware of the center of our orbits in that our orbits are the paths we travel in life through work, play, and relationships. We can make decisions about what to watch on TV, what books to read, what kind of job is best, where to invest our money, how to vote, and who we spend our time with based on our center of gravity—the thing that pulls us back to our core. Some might refer to this center of gravity as values or convictions, the significant principles that guide our actions over our lifetimes. As Christians, we should center these values around the gravity of God's uncompromising and unparalleled love and truth.

God's Love

God's love is such an integral part of His character (as are His other attributes) that they are inextricably linked in Scripture. And we, as His followers, are meant to be characterized by that love as well.

> *Beloved, let us love one another, because love comes from God. Everyone who loves has been born of God and knows God. Whoever does not love does not know God, because* **God is love***.*
>
> (1 John 4:7-8, NIV)

> *So we have come to know and to believe the love that God has for us.* **God is love***, and whoever abides in love abides in God, and God abides in him.*
>
> (1 John 4:16, ESV)

God's unconditional love gives our lives meaning, informs our attitudes and actions, and motivates us to become the best version of ourselves in the world, knowing that we have value and are loved and accepted.

When that love is the center of gravity that continually pulls us closer to God's presence, keeping us from thoughts, words, and behavior that would contradict or compromise our relationship with Him or with others, we're able to live, work, and play in a consistent orbit in the universe, where we can shine like stars as we move. Spontaneity and unexpected circumstances will undoubtedly assail us from time to time, but those seasons of life won't knock us out of orbit so that we are flailing around in space with no frame of reference for who we are or whose we are. God's love anchors us.

Confidence in God's love will keep us from looking for affirmation in unhealthy activities and relationships, as well. When I am secure in the love that God has for me, which is based on His character and not mine, then I'm full and free to give to others and not to look to them to tell me I'm important or valuable. Losing sight of this or not fully understanding it in the first place causes us to date men who don't respect us or treat us well.

We may drink too much or develop obsessions around eating or exercising so that we can live up to the standards of the world's image of beauty and value. As professional women, we may work long hours and compromise our relationships or health to get a promotion, close a deal, or make more money. When we don't know or when we forget how much we're loved by God—the One who made us carefully and wonderfully unique—we will continue to search for that affirmation and love from people, achievements, and images around us. God has already proven His love when He chose us to be adopted into His family and made a way for us to have a relationship with Him through Jesus. When we fully understand God's love for us, we will want to stay in orbit around His presence. Then our consistent orbit will be around the things and people that please Him and make us more like Him.

Acknowledging and assimilating God's love into our lives is the heart of knowing our identity as Christians. God is love, and God defines us with His love.

You have likely read Luke 3:21-22 before. I have, too. But every time I read a passage I've read before, I'm different than the last time I read it. God has changed me. My circumstances have changed. My perspective has changed. Therefore, I trust that God has a new layer or a different revelation for me.

> *When all the people were being baptized, Jesus was baptized, too. And as he was praying, heaven was opened and the Holy Spirit descended on him in bodily form like a dove. And a voice came from heaven: "You are my Son, whom I love; with you I am well pleased."*

If you look at the gospel accounts that contain this scene you will notice the same thing we see here: God was pleased with Jesus and loved him before he ever did a miracle or taught an impressive sermon. His ministry began after his baptism and 40 days in the wilderness. The pattern is the same for us. God wants us to know who we are and it always begins with words of love and pleasure from a Father. When we strip away the superficial layers of our identity and depend on God to tell us who we are, we have so much more than we could ever come up with on our own.

If I'm walking in the identity for which God has created me and wants me to live, then I'm free to pursue the goals in life that He has for me and I don't need to take from other people to feel good about myself or fight for my rights. Nor do I need to feel threatened by someone else's ideas or accomplishments. I don't need to live in insecurity wondering if what I'm doing will ever be good enough. I can let God direct me and fill me, and I can then give to others from the abundance He has given me. On the other hand, if I'm unsure of the identity God has for me, or if I lose sight of it periodically, I am forced to fill myself and identify myself with things that will change or not last for eternity. This leads me to compare myself to others or put others down so that I can feel good about myself. Or I just keep going and going and going so I don't have to stop and wonder if what I'm doing is enough. Some do this with buying things for the house. Some never stop working, hoping that achievements will tell them who they are.

People use a fake ID to pretend they're someone they're not. And usually it's not for a noble purpose. God wants us to be the people He's created us to be when He knit us together in our mother's wombs, chromosome by chromosome, and that's how He wants us to shine in the world: exactly the way He made us. He loves us that way!

When my son Charlie was little I used to ask him, "Do I love you because you're smart?" "Do I love you because you're handsome?" He knew the answer was no. I would ask him, "Why do I love you?" And without hesitation, he would answer, "You love me because I'm Charlie." Yes! I wanted him to always know that regardless of his performance, appearance, or behavior, I loved him because he's mine.

When he got to be in high school, I would still play that game with him once in a while. When he did well at a diving meet or got good grades, I'd ask again, "Do I love you because you got an A?" Of course, his teen attitude was burgeoning by this time, and his responses were less enthusiastic, but he was still able to articulate that I loved him simply because he was mine, often by mumbling, "You love me cuz I'm Charlie." In both those seasons it was pretty easy to play the game and to love him for lots of reasons. He was easy to love, had great friends, good grades, and yes, he was stunningly handsome, in this mother's opinion.

There were a couple of seasons, however, when it was more challenging. When Charlie was going through chemotherapy and taking steroids during his cancer treatment, he didn't look like himself, act like himself, or even smell like himself. If you've been through cancer treatment or known someone who's been through it, you know how chemotherapy drugs and steroids can jack you up. Also, when Charlie was deepest into his drug use, he didn't resemble the handsome, compliant, articulate boy I had raised. In both cases drugs were altering his appearance and his demeanor. It was more important than ever during those times that I reminded myself that I didn't love Charlie because of any of the easy reasons. I love him because he's mine.

That's the message God has for us. The crux of His love message. He loves us because we're His. Anything else we rely on will let us down and leave us wanting. From a solid understanding of who God made us to be, we can shine like stars in this crooked and warped generation and show the universe what it means to hold out the word of life.

Sometimes that's a hard concept to grasp or remember. Because God's love (and faithfulness, righteousness, grace, and mercy) is beyond the realm of physical attributes, it may be a challenge to internalize what feel like obscure concepts. We can think about a human being's hug or a smile. We know what support, comfort, and companionship feel like in our relationships with people. But it's sometimes harder with the all-powerful, invisible God we serve. When that love feels elusive or we need reminders of God's character in other ways, there is a place to ground us and establish our orbit in another way.

God's Truth

The Bible is full of stories of people whose lives have radically changed because of learning, understanding, and assimilating the words of God's law. These transformations aren't just limited to the characters in Scripture, either. It's true in my life, in the lives of many people I know, and it's probably true in your life, too. God's Word—the Bible—contains the inspired and unchanging love letter and instruction book sent to us by our Father, God the Creator. He intended for us to immerse ourselves in these words so that we could know Him better and live in a way that best reflects Him to the world. To shine in the darkness, if you will.

Paul encouraged the Romans to let Scripture transform them when he wrote: *"...everything that was written in the past was written to teach us, so that through endurance and the encouragement of the Scriptures, we might have hope"* (Romans 15:4). That endurance, hope, and encouragement to live with truth at the center of our lives comes from knowing what the Bible says. In order to avail ourselves of that wisdom we need to read and understand Scripture. Not because it's a way to impress others or make God love us more, but because it's the fuel we need to live out loud and shine in the universe.

There are as many ways to approach Scripture for learning, understanding, and life change as there are personality types and preferences. You may listen to podcasts by favorite pastors; you may enjoy a morning devotional with small, bite-sized doses of Scripture for the day; you may join a group study in your neighborhood or church; you may read through all 66 books in a year with a chart. *How* you study matters, but that you study at all is far more crucial. We can't live out God's truth if we don't know it. We may remember snippets or stories from Sunday School or high school youth group, but the bottom line is this: if we are not consistently and currently consuming the Bible, we are not growing. Without Scripture as a litmus test for other voices we hear, we can never be certain that what we're hearing is truth.

Here are some methods of studying the Bible that may appeal to you.

Inductive Study

Several revered and prolific Bible teachers and authors have put together studies on books of the Bible based on a study method called inductive Bible study. This method of studying Scripture uses three specific steps to move from being unfamiliar with the passage being studied to having it apply to our lives practically and then having an impact spiritually. These are the three steps:

OBSERVATION

INTERPRETATION

APPLICATION

Observation is merely a list of facts and details and patterns that are seen in any given section of the Bible. There may or may not be any spiritual significance to the observations; they are merely facts that catch our attention. At this beginning phase of Bible study, it's important to look for things like repeated phrases or words, descriptions that go from specific to general or vice versa, and things that may be true-to-life. We're simply asking, "What do I see?"

Interpretation, for the purpose of inductive Bible study, is looking for the meaning behind the facts. This may include getting some historical context or looking up specific words to better understand them. Because not all the books of the Bible were meant to be read the same way, we need to know how to approach and interpret each one. The books of 1st and 2nd Kings are historical narratives, explaining actual events and people who lived thousands of years ago. We wouldn't read them the same way we would read the last book of the Bible, Revelation, because that book is filled with allegories and visions that aren't meant to be taken literally in the same sense that battle details are. In this phase of study, we ask, "What does it mean?"

Application is the final and most personal and spiritual step in this method of study. This is when we finally get to ask how the passage applies to my life. Is there sin in my life that needs to be addressed? Should I be praying for someone specifically? Do my attitudes, thoughts, words, or actions require adjustment?

When we start reading the Bible for what applies to us first, we miss the point of Scripture, which is to reveal God Himself. He is the main character of the Bible, not us. So we look for Him, and He will reveal Himself and what He wants to do in our lives.

Here's an example of how you might work through a passage of Scripture with this method. Let's take some verses from Lamentations.

> *I remember my affliction and my wandering,*
> *the bitterness and the gall.*
> *I well remember them,*
> *and my soul is downcast within me.*
> *Yet this I call to mind*
> *and therefore I have hope:*
>
> *Because of the LORD's great love we are not consumed,*
> *for his compassions never fail.*
> *They are new every morning;*
> *great is your faithfulness.*
> *I say to myself, "The LORD is my portion;*
> *therefore I will wait for him."*
>
> *The LORD is good to those whose hope is in him,*
> *to the one who seeks him;*
> *it is good to wait quietly*
> *for the salvation of the LORD.*
> (Lamentations 3:19-26)

My **observations** include the fact that Jeremiah is the author and he also wrote the preceding eponymous book of the Bible. I see that he has been afflicted and is depressed, and since I've read the book of Jeremiah, I know that's kind of a theme with him. He has been mistreated and is suffering. But there's a contrast between the first section of this passage and the second section. The first is stating facts of his circumstances and his consequent feelings. The second section, starting with verse 21—yet—is filled with spiritual truths. In those spiritual truths, I would list the following about God:

* He has great love and is compassionate. (verse 22)

* He is faithful. (verse 23)

* He is good to those who hope in Him. (verse 25)

I also see that Jeremiah is telling himself some things, as if directing his emotions by appealing to his logic.

What else do you see?

The **interpretation** piece of this passage could include things like the fact that I see an example of someone who is emotionally compromised by his circumstances, but who chooses to reflect on and remember what He knows is true about God. This is a good practice because God's truth is more reliable and more consistent than any circumstances or emotions in life. And I know something about this period of Old Testament history (between 586 and 575 B.C.) so I know that the circumstances were dire. The Jews had been taken away from their holy city, Jerusalem, and were captives in Babylon, where they had to learn a new language, a new culture, and be far away from the temple, which had been destroyed. Jeremiah is talking about real and weighty circumstances caused by God to discipline His children.

Finally, I'm ready to apply some of these truths to my own life in the **application** piece. As I'm writing this, there are three men digging a hole under my office because we have no water pressure. They suspect a leak under the house. Tomorrow is Thanksgiving and I'm hosting. I'm overwhelmed and saddened by my circumstances. And I'm tempted to add, "just like Jeremiah" until I remember what, exactly, Jeremiah was facing. Then

I tell myself to lighten up. I also tell myself, "Because of the LORD's great love we are not consumed, for his compassions never fail." I can remind myself that God is powerful and compassionate and cares about my measly little plumbing problem as much as He cares about starving children and war-torn countries because He is omnipresent and omnipotent; my little problems don't compromise His power or His love because taking care of the world is easy for Him! I will trust God with my Thanksgiving dinner and with my life because He loves me and is "good to those whose hope is in him."

Filter Questions

A more generic way of approaching Scripture is to have what I call filter questions. I've seen several versions of these by several reputable Christian organizations, and I've come up with my own. They all serve the same purpose: take any section of Scripture and interact with it on an intellectual and spiritual level.

Here are questions I ask:

What do I learn about God from this passage?
What questions do I have?
What is challenging me?
What connections do I see to other things in Scripture?
What can I pray about?
How is God asking me to apply this?

These questions are simply tools to give a framework to any section of the Bible we may be reading as we go through any book we choose. We can begin by asking God to reveal what's important; the condition of our hearts is important when we read Scripture. We may also want to research introductory or background information that might be helpful to understanding the context of Scripture. It's easier to understand the deeper meaning of something when we start with the basic meaning of the words and the intent of the authors.

These questions can be applied to the same verses we just studied inductively. What do you learn about God from Jeremiah's lament? What questions do you have and where can you find the answers? A Bible commentary? Google? Other passages of Scripture? And so on and so on.

S.O.A.P.

S.O.A.P. is a helpful acronym for reading through Scripture that achieves similar goals to the methods I've already mentioned. And I find it hard to resist an acronym as a mnemonic device!

S—The S stands for **Scripture.** What is the passage you're reading? Sometimes this is assigned by a church group doing the exercise together; other times it's simply chosen by what interests you.

O—The O is for **Observation**. This is similar to the Inductive Bible Study Method in that you're simply seeing what the passage contains. Is there repetition? Who is writing? Who is the audience?

A—This is for **Application.** After seeing some facts and details about a given passage, God's Holy Spirit may be prompting some response in you. This often occurs when you feel uneasy, angry, excited, or confused by a passage. All Scripture is God-breathed and useful (2 Timothy 3:16-17), but not all Scripture will affect us the same way each time we read it. God's Spirit is a teacher and He will light up passages for us that are meant to be more significant and personal.

P—This is for **Prayer.** Once you've familiarized yourself with a part of Scripture and you see how it applies to you, a natural and healthy response is to talk to God about it in prayer. This may entail confessing sin He's revealed or it may mean interceding for a specific person God has put on your heart. It may also be as simple as asking God for more clarity on something you've read.

Again, take the verses from Lamentations 3 and use this method to glean even more insight than you may have from the previous methods.

What I like about all of these methods is that they not only engage us intellectually by making more of the Bible familiar to us; they also invite us to engage with God on a more personal and spiritual level so that transformation occurs. Let's look at an example.

Read the following passage from the gospel of Luke:

> *Now he [Jesus] was teaching in one of the synagogues on the Sabbath. And behold, there was a woman who had had a disabling spirit for eighteen years. She was bent over and could not fully straighten herself. When Jesus saw her, he called her over and said to her, "Woman, you are freed from your disability." And he laid his hands on her, and immediately she was made straight, and she glorified God.*
>
> (Luke 13:10-13 ESV)

We can read the verses before and after this passage to get some context further explaining what Jesus was doing at the time. We can ask ourselves if this healing is similar to or different from other healings Jesus did in the gospels. We can read various translations to see whether this "disabling spirit" was psychosomatic or arthritis or something else. We can explore the theological implications of the Jews who criticized Jesus for healing her. All of these are fascinating and important.

Ultimately, though, once we have explored the word meanings, historical context, and theological implications, there will be a time when we read this passage and ask ourselves what God wants to do in us. Or what God *has* done in us. There is a phrase here that resonated with me when I heard it in a sermon recently: *"Woman, you are freed..."* If Jesus is the same yesterday, today, and forever (Hebrews 13:8), then He is able to free me from things that weigh me down. That may take the form of anxiety, comparison, depression, or physical disease. He sees me, He calls to me, and He wants to touch me in a way that allows me to stand up straight and be the woman

He created me to be! Then my natural response will be to give Him glory! I will shine most brilliantly and most beautifully when it's in response to God's love and truth unleashed in my life! Woman, you can be free!

There are many people and organizations that encourage the sound practices of meditation, visualization, and being still in the morning. There is evidence—scientific and anecdotal—pointing to these practices being closely linked to productivity and success in achieving goals. I am fully convinced, however, that what we are meditating on and how we choose the source of our goals and inspiration matter more than any structure or method we choose to implement. If it's based on anything other than the absolute truth of Scripture, we are choosing sources that may not be in alignment with God's truth. More importantly, by reading books about God or other sources of inspiration that are spiritual but not Christian, we may be tempted to believe incremental lies that will ultimately lead us to the kind of selfish ambition and watered-down faith that the Bible warns us about.

Reading books *about* the Bible is no substitute for reading the Bible itself.

Talking to people about what *they've* read in the Bible or heard in a sermon is no substitute for reading the Bible itself.

Having read some of the Bible *at some point* in your spiritual journey is no substitute for reading the Bible on a regular basis now.

We may read other things *in addition* to the Bible; I'm a huge fan of reading and learning and keeping current in professional industry literature, current events, fiction, and books about the Christian living. But reading books and articles about the Bible should come *after* we've delved into the original source itself. We read the Bible because it's God's letter to us about Him. Then we can enjoy other materials that add to what the Holy Spirit has already revealed to us in reading Scripture for ourselves. **There is simply no substitute for regular and systematic intake of Scripture in order to know God and to grow spiritually.** And like any other spiritual discipline, starting with something is better than nothing. We do it out of obedience and in response to a loving, powerful God who has snatched us from an empty life centered on ourselves and eternal destiny of destruction, rescuing us and appointing us to eternal life in glory with Him. Not because we have to out of some sense of drudgery or obligation, but in response to who God is and what He's done for us.

Look at these verses from Paul's first letter to the Thessalonian Christians as an example of making sure our orbit is centered on God's love and truth. I've included two different translations to give us more to think about.

> *Do not put out the Spirit's fire; do not treat prophecies with contempt. Test everything. Hold on to the good. Avoid every kind of evil.*
>
> (1 Thessalonians 5:19-22, NIV)

> *Do not quench the Spirit. Do not despise prophecies, but test everything; hold fast to what is good. Abstain from every from of evil.*
>
> (1 Thessalonians 5:19-22, ESV)

This is an example of an orbit. As called children of God (not in darkness, but children of light, as in 1 Thessalonians 5:5), we're meant to live by God's standards, which are His provision and protection for us and the best way to be close to Him and experience Him. These verses are an example of the kind of orbit that's best for us. The life that experiences more of God's glory. This chapter has several guidelines for living, all designed with God's love and truth as the center of gravity.

Verse 16—*Rejoice always.* Why? Because God has sent Jesus to redeem me, forgive me, and make me whole.

Verse 17—*Pray without ceasing.* Why? Because God loves me and cares about what I care about. And because I can! Jesus made a way for me to enter God's presence.

Verse 18—*Give thanks.* Why? There's so much to be thankful for! Even in the midst of boring or challenging seasons, I can look at my spiritual state and all that God has done for me and be thankful.

Verse 19—*Don't quench the Spirit*. Why? Because the Spirit's job is to sanctify me—to transform me to look more and more like Jesus. The imagery here is of flames. (NIV—*"Don't put out the Spirit's fire."*) The Spirit came to the early church at Pentecost like flames, and we read about the Spirit as a fire in other parts of Scripture. When the Spirit wants to get into the deepest part of me to change me and speak God's words of life over my life, I want to let Him consume me so there's nothing left of my old nature, but what remains is what God is doing in me to shine in the world around me. That fire in me is like the nuclear fusion in a star's core, emanating light into the surrounding darkness. I don't want to put that out!

Verses 20-21—*Don't treat prophecies with contempt, but test everything.* How? I need to know the truth of God's Word to be able to discern which words people speak are true! And I need to be humble enough to keep going to God for the truth, not becoming arrogant by bringing my own views to what I read in Scripture. When the latter happens, it makes the orbit around my own opinion instead of what God is saying to me through His Word.

Verses 21-22—*Hold on to the good; avoid evil.* Why? Who wants to run toward evil if we say we love and follow Jesus? But how can we know what is good and what is evil without the absolute standard of God's truth?

These are just a few examples of how we can fix our orbit around God's truth and love. But how can we be aware of our orbit around what's true about God if we don't know it in the first place?

Our orbit is our way of living—everything we do. If we examine our behavior, our center of gravity will reveal itself, but are we intentional about it? Do we orbit around our own tiny ideas? Or do we orbit around God's eternal, unchanging ones? If we claim to orbit around God's ideas, what do we base it on? What we learned in Sunday school or youth group years ago? Sermons once a week? Or do we orient our lives around what God reveals to us corporately AND individually through His Word?

As I read these verses in 1 Thessalonians, there are some questions that come to mind for me to apply to my life:

* **What's my general attitude in life?** Do I rejoice and give thanks, doing everything without complaining or arguing? Or do I grumble and focus on the negative, making myself the center of my orbit?

* **Am I doing anything in my life that might quench the Spirit?** Am I ignoring His voice and impeding the sanctification process? The Holy Spirit is the One who makes me shine!

* **Am I informing myself about God consistently enough that I can test things I hear from others?** This is how I establish and maintain my orbit.

* **Am I fiercely devoted to what is good and equally passionate about eschewing anything that is negative and harmful to my relationship with God?** In other words, are my standards God's standards or am I creating my own based on society's or what feels good in the moment?

Knowing the Bible for ourselves will give us the confidence to live out loud and shine in a dark world. It will also allow us to discern truth from error when someone is teaching us.

Several years ago, after I had spoken at a women's retreat, the wrap-up session began with women sharing what they had learned and what God had revealed to them during our time together. One woman who had been in one of the small groups I sat in on got up to share that she didn't believe me when I had said that the Bible tells us that God was grieved over making mankind because He saw that every inclination of man's heart was only evil all the time. She stood in front of 50 women, looked directly at me, and said, "I didn't believe you. Then I looked it up." She then looked at the rest of the group and said, "It's in there." (Genesis 6, if you're interested...)

When she finished sharing, I addressed the group and commended that woman for being like the Bereans Luke described in Acts as being *"more noble-minded than the Thessalonians, for they received the message with great eagerness and examined the Scriptures every day to see if these teachings were true"* (Acts 17:11, NIV). Just because someone quotes a verse or stands in front of a church or a group or in a podcast does not mean that you should accept the message unquestioningly. Even if what a speaker or teacher says is true, knowing the Bible ourselves will bring added depth and context and personal application for our lives that will enrich our relationship with God and with other people.

I have a friend named Rochelle, who expressed to me some frustrations she was having in church on Sundays. She didn't understand the sermons because she didn't know the stories and characters that the pastor was referring to in his messages. She had gone to church for years but didn't know how to access the power of the Bible for herself. So we started meeting together on a regular basis, exploring how the Bible was put together as well as points of relevance and methods for study. Over the course of the year we met together, the characters and stories came alive for her and she gained confidence in how she could have conversations with her children about spiritual issues. We applied the Bible to parenting, worry, money, politics, friendships, marriage, and more.

You can't imagine how excited I was to read her words recently as she reflected on that experience.

> *For years I attended several different churches and often walked away not fully understanding what the message meant. The pastor would reference different passages from the Bible and I wouldn't know the context of the passage, let alone how it applied to the message as a whole or to my life. It left me frustrated and confused... I now have an understanding of the meaning of the Old Testament, the New Testament, the authors, and most importantly how God, Jesus, and the Holy Spirit are connected. Now when I attend a church service I am able to apply the context of the verse to the message itself. I know where to look within the Bible and understand the meaning as it relates to the author and time period in which it was written. Further, now that I understand how the Bible is organized and know more about each of the authors, I have a better interpretation of the context of a passage rather than taking the pastor's opinion verbatim. I can decipher the*

information based on my knowledge combined with that of the message being delivered. This has brought a whole new level of spirituality to my life. Rather than focusing on what I don't know, I can focus on the message itself, how it relates to my understanding of that verse in the Bible, and best of all, how God is working in my life as it relates to that message.

It's exciting to witness the transformation that happens in a person's life when she engages at an intellectual level with Scripture AND a deeper spiritual level that exposes her to God's love.

I apply this concept of regularly checking in with Scripture when I hear Sunday messages, as well. When I was on a mission trip to Bulgaria recently, I listened to a message a pastor delivered about Moses. One of the points she made was that we should allow God to drive our lives and trust Him to know the way and take us there. One aspect of the message didn't sit well with me, and I wasn't sure if the speaker was emphasizing a part of the passage I didn't remember or simply extrapolating what she thought were thoughts Moses may have had about his situation. So the next morning, I read through the passage she had referenced (Exodus 3) to see what God had to show me. As I read, it became clear to me that the speaker had been doing some interpretation that I wouldn't have necessarily picked up on, but it wasn't wrong information. That was comforting, but what had a more profound impact on me was what God revealed to me in reading a familiar passage again in a new place. God's words to Moses— *I've heard the cries of my people; I've seen their misery; I've come to rescue them*—took on new context as the Holy Spirit reminded me of the children we had seen the day before in a small village of recently bulldozed houses. "You've seen and heard their misery, Lord!" I cried out in prayer. "When will you come rescue them?" God made a passage of Scripture I'd read many times before personal and relevant because of a sermon I'd heard and was curious about.

Our personal understanding of Scripture will keep us grounded in what we believe when others are teaching, and it will enrich our relationship with God when we see His glory and personal touches in the way He reveals

His Word to us. When we are frustrated with a sermon series at church or are tempted to be critical of the teaching on Sundays, it may be because the only thing we're hearing from God is that message. (We might still have opinions about the style of delivery or certain points made in a message, but even then, we can ask God in our private times with Him what we should take to heart and what we should release.) On the other hand, if we're spending consistent time in God's Word on our own, hearing His voice guide us into His truth so His Spirit can change us and show us more of who He is, we'll hear a Sunday message with a unique and timely perspective that only comes from the fullness of relationship with Him all week long.

In the same way that we would question the nutritional wisdom of only eating one meal a week, we have to question the effectiveness and spiritual wisdom of only "being fed" by a pastor's sermon once a week. We are meant to be feeding ourselves! And if you think about it, you're not just eating one meal a week and expecting it to sustain you for the next seven days; you're doing the spiritual equivalent of eating food that's already been chewed! Why settle for listening to the pastor recount *his* experience with God when you can have your own? Not only will Sunday sermons take on new meaning and have more relevance and profound impact in our lives when we engage with Scripture regularly, but experiencing the Bible consistently will also more naturally inform our conversations and decisions Monday through Saturday. God's Word is inspirational AND practical in our lives, allowing us to remain in a consistent orbit around His truth and love, like stars are held together by gravity and orbit around the center of the universe.

Questions for Discussion or Application:

+ Read 1 John 3:1. What does it tell you about God's love in your life? How can you appropriate this verse and others like it to encourage you when it's hard to feel God's love?

+ Try one of the methods mentioned in this chapter and use it to read and understand this passage in James. You may want to write out your observations on a separate sheet of paper.

My dear brothers and sisters, take note of this: Everyone should be quick to listen, slow to speak and slow to become angry, because human anger does not produce the righteousness that God desires. Therefore, get rid of all moral filth and the evil that is so prevalent and humbly accept the word planted in you, which can save you.

Do not merely listen to the word, and so deceive yourselves. Do what it says. Anyone who listens to the word but does not do what it says is like someone who looks at his face in a mirror and, after looking at himself, goes away and immediately forgets what he looks like. But whoever looks intently into the perfect law that gives freedom, and continues in it—not forgetting what they have heard, but doing it—they will be blessed in what they do.

(James 1:19-25)

Chapter 5

Flaming Out

Stars can be beautiful and a shining example of consistency from here on Earth with their constant and twinkling presence overhead. However, from our vantage point so many miles away, we don't see the white-hot effect of that nuclear fusion that fuels the stars. While we're enjoying the stellar sparkle in the night sky, there are also more toxic and dramatic activities occurring that only scientists with telescopes can see.

Early in the morning on September 6th, 2017, the Sun released two powerful solar flares from a large spot on its surface. These blasts of radiation, three hours apart, were stronger than any recorded in years and caused radio blackouts and other interruptions of low frequency communication. And although these examples were particularly noticeable, these dramatic pulses from our Sun—and other stars—are not uncommon. They occur when the "sun's magnetic field... twists up and reconnects, blasting energy outward and superheating the solar surface."[1] Sometimes radiation emanates from the Sun, while other times there may be a release of energetic plasma, or particles, that travel into space. This is called a coronal mass ejection.

In 2005 scientists spotted a stellar flare that may have been the largest ever detected. If this star had been our Sun, instead of located 135 light-years away, in the constellation Pegasus, it would have triggered a mass extinction of Earth, as it released energy equivalent to about 50 trillion atomic bombs. Scientists believe that because this star is part of a binary orbit—two stars orbiting around each other—the speed and difference in mass between the stars may have caused it to be more active than our sun.

But since II Pegasi is so far away, we can sleep peacefully at night, knowing that our solar system's center is far less volatile.[2]

Stars emit toxic gamma rays when things get too hot, and so do we.

As stars, the light we want to shine in the world is meant to be like the most attractive lighting at a make-up counter, reflecting the best of our features in the mirror. We want our light to be like a warm bonfire. Like a soft white 60-watt bulb. That's the kind of light that draws people to the God we serve. What happens when we let sin get the best of us is that our light becomes garish and offensive, causing those around us to look away, shielding their eyes from harsh and unattractive brightness. It's too much. And it hurts.

Sin in our lives can have toxic effects not unlike the ones scientists have seen happening on the Sun and other stars in space. Problems arise when we let sin get the best of us, lashing out in anger, choosing selfish ambition over selfless service to others, or inadvertently hurting those around us with our words or actions.

While it's easy to see the harmful effects of words spoken in anger, we're not often eager or willing to call it what it is: sin. We can apologize and ask for forgiveness, but it takes time for the relationship to recover. Marriages can fall apart because of infidelity, but they can also suffer from lying, anger, and contempt, all of which go against God's standards for His children's behavior. All of these can be labelled as sin.

Even our private sins have a negative effect on those who love us. An example that affects many is pornography. The world will say that boys will be boys and that they should be allowed to have their fun in this now all but ubiquitous form of entertainment. But I have heard stories from woman after woman who describe how they are suffering the effects because their husbands have been engaged in this insidiously destructive addiction; they are emotionally hurt, financially depleted, or worse. Our sin offends God and hurts others. And it damages the light we shine into the world.

As we learn and experience more and more of God's truth and presence in our lives, the Holy Spirit will reveal areas of sin that need to change by His power. And as the Holy Spirit reveals those areas, we, like stars, will burn off those outer layers of our old lives. In that process, however, our sin may cause flare ups and emit harsh gamma rays into the world, hurting the people around us. We may be tempted in those times to excuse our behavior or blame others for bringing it out in us, but we alone are responsible for our sinful reactions regardless of the temptation or circumstances that cause them.

If we let them, these times can provide opportunities for us to discover what only God can do—transform our hearts—and what only we can do—confess our sin, repent, and seek mercy and forgiveness. Confessing sin is agreeing with God that our behavior doesn't line up with His standards. Repenting is the act of turning away from that behavior because we want to please God. Talking to Him about the behaviors that aren't consistent with His character allows us to receive mercy and forgiveness, allowing us to experience more of God's glory and live life the way we were meant to.

This is why we shine so brightly sometimes and other times... not so much.

I see three main causes of this disconnect between the fullness of shining the way we were created to shine and the sin that hides our lights under baskets and causes pain to those around us.

1. We aren't spending time with God so it's harder for Him to influence our thoughts and actions.

2. We don't know God's Word so we aren't living by His standards.

3. We choose to hang on to sin and it disallows us from hearing God's voice and receiving His blessings.

God's Influence

Look at Acts 4:13

> *When they saw the courage of Peter and John and realized that they were unschooled, ordinary men, they were astonished and they took note that these men had been with Jesus.*

People noticed that Peter and John had been with Jesus. This influenced their words and their actions. When we spend a lot of time with a friend or a sister, we sometimes notice that we pick up each other's idiosyncrasies or language. People might say, "You sure are Judy's daughter. You move your hands the same way!" I noticed at a family retreat years ago that my mother-in-law and her sister laugh the same way and hold their food the same way when they eat. My best friend tilts her head to the side and talks out of one side of her mouth when she's saying something she deems saucy or clever. Now I find myself doing it, too!

If we don't spend time with God, listening for His truth and voice in our lives, it's not going to surprise anyone that there's nothing in our lives that looks like Him. We are influenced by the people and the environments around us. That's a fact.

At the end of the same mission trip to Bulgaria I mentioned earlier, I found myself, on the last day, sitting in an apartment with a creative artist who makes leather handbags and other beautiful leather accessories. We chatted and I purchased a few items. Then, as our transaction had ended and she was going to walk me back to the metro station, I asked if I could pray for her business and her marriage. She agreed and we got to have a spiritual finish to our delightful time together. I prayed that God would bring her new ideas for products and new clients. I asked God to give her and her husband joy as they continued to bless others in their community. I don't usually end my time with people like that, but because I had been with a group of people praying day and evening for people whose homes had been bulldozed to the ground, people who didn't have jobs, and for schools with teens at risk of being trafficked for labor and sex, I had spent significantly more time with God, depending on Him and looking to Him, than I do in a normal week at home. I was an ordinary woman who had been spending more time with Jesus, so my reactions to things changed. And I liked it!

God's Standards

We can't grow in obedience to God if we don't know what His Word says. And consequences from our disobedience will be present in our lives even if we don't know what we've done wrong in the same way that a police officer will still give you a ticket for speeding even if you claim not to know what the speed limit was on the road where he caught you! Without an anchor of truth to guide my actions and attitudes, I'm going to live life as if I'm being *"tossed back and forth by the waves, blown here and there by every wind of teaching and by the cunning and craftiness of people in their deceitful scheming"* (Ephesians 4:14). Without knowing God's Word, I have no frame of reference for what goodness or truth may be, and it's likely that I will be deceived or feckless in my belief system. It's possible to have our minds so open that we fail to recognize inconsistencies and absolute truth in our search for relevancy and tolerance. Just because someone says it's true doesn't make it so. Walking with Jesus in love and obedience necessitates knowing what the truth of His Word is so we can walk in it. *"Teach me your way, O LORD, that I may walk in your truth"* (Psalm 86:11).

Without a clear understanding of and ability to articulate truths from Scripture, it's likely we'll believe the most persuasive person in the room, compromise our values as we lose sight of them, or shrink back from speaking up about our opinions on everything from politics to pop culture because we aren't sure of what we believe or why. In this crooked and warped generation, the consequences for speaking our convictions can be staggering, but holding firmly to the word of life has never been more important.

I recently became involved in helping a nonprofit organization in Seattle called R.E.S.T. They help provide hope and resources for women who are caught in various aspects of the sex industry. My husband and I support them financially, and we've had fundraising events at our home. I also have begun to look at what role society plays in perpetuating a culture that demeans women and makes light of aspects of this tragedy as opposed to all I've read in Scripture that talks about how much value God places on His children.

On a friend's Facebook page a while ago, someone posted a fun game to determine what your stripper name would be if you combined something like the name of the street you grew up on and the color underwear you had on at the moment. Because of my work with R.E.S.T. and my time reading the Bible and learning to understand God's heart for His daughters, I saw this post in a new light. It wasn't funny to think of young women who are so broken that the only way they see value in themselves is with their bodies and seduction. Whether by choice or coercion, exotic dancing and prostitution are manifestations of the brokenness of individuals and society as a whole.

I read verses like, *"Speak up for those who cannot speak for themselves... defend the rights of the poor and needy"* (Proverbs 31:8-9) and others that speak of God's standards and love for His people, and I can't look at society the same way.

Because of my growing understanding and convictions around this, I replied to my friend's post by writing something about this industry not always being a choice for women and that it can be damaging and demeaning. I suggested that we consider others' situations when posting things like this as some women are struggling to discover their worth, and some are doing it because they're being forced to. I don't remember the exact words I used, but as soon as she read it, she removed the post and apologized to everyone in another post for being potentially insensitive. I then texted her privately to see if a follow-up conversation was needed to clear the air between us, and she assured me that it was a good thing that I brought that perspective to her attention and that we were fine.

My time listening to God, reading His Word, and spending time with other people to gain a wider perspective has changed how I view the world. And those convictions are profound enough to be articulated in conversations. Living out loud means that I can speak my convictions with confidence, but that I will also take into account others' feeling and the inestimable value their lives have because God loves them and created them.

We will grow in confidence AND in our love for others as we let the power of God's Word penetrate more and more deeply into our hearts. This is the nuclear fusion the world needs to see as light in the darkness! The absence of that influence allows us to gravitate toward the least desirable characteristics and patterns in our lives; that's when sin keeps us from shining the way we were meant to shine.

God's Voice and Blessings

Instead of hating the evil I do, I embrace it, give in to it, or justify it with excuses. This is hard to admit, and it often takes a close friend or spouse to bring it to the surface, but it can't be ignored as a potential cause of darkness when we say we want to shine. It's easier to remain connected to people and situations that feed our immediate needs for comfort, security, or pleasure than it is to break away and choose the more satisfying long-term activities and environments that God prescribes for us. And it's easier to justify my anger because someone hurt me than it is to ask both the offended person and God for forgiveness and change my behavior.

There are personality traits that we may ask people to accept in us: I laugh too loudly or I like cheesy movies. Sin doesn't fall into this category. No one gets to say, "I'm afraid you have to accept me the way I am; I just lie a lot." That is sin. Instead, we ask God and those we trust to help us live lives that reflect God's character by walking in love and obedience.

Struggling against sin is human; rationalizing it or giving into it is disobedience. And it makes it hard to shine.

If I had cherished sin in my heart,
the Lord would not have listened;
but God has surely listened
and has heard my prayer.
(Psalm 66:18-19)

When we aren't shining the way we say we want to, it's probably because we're living disconnected, ignorant, or disobedient lives. And the answer isn't just to buckle down and try harder. I'm not talking about legalistically jumping through religious hoops to avoid God's punishment or earn His approval. That's the opposite of the gospel. He loves you because you're His!

It's not about DOING more for the sake of impressing others. I'm saying that when we spend time away from God, allowing the influences of this world to speak into our lives and control us, there will be consequences. It will show up in our attitudes, our actions, and our relationships. And when we don't take responsibility to participate fully in the transformation process, we have no one to blame but ourselves.

Have you noticed seasons on your life when there's a correlation between bad choices and lack of time thinking about *"whatever is true, whatever is noble, whatever is right, whatever is pure, whatever is lovely, whatever is admirable... excellent, or praiseworthy"* (Philippians 4:8)? Is temptation harder to resist when you can't remember the last time you opened your Bible? Is it easier to justify movie choices, dating choices, or conversations you participate in when God has become a peripheral aspect of your life? Or maybe you've see the opposite scenario, one in which you know you're in a relationship that's not what God would want so you purposely avoid Him. These examples aren't meant to make us feel ashamed because we aren't following the rules; God's not waiting for us to misstep so He can smack our knuckles with a ruler. God doesn't punish us for not spending enough time reading the Bible or going to church, but there is certainly a cause-and-effect relationship between our time focused on Him and the influence He has in our priorities and choices.

My best friend went through some painful circumstances several years ago, and God revealed Himself to her in her struggle and pain. We spoke often about how she was processing things and what God was telling her. Her struggle was both with the sin that others had committed and her own sin in response. She was willing to look at both.

Here's how Julianna describes it:

> *I walked with Jesus for many years relying on Sunday sermons and Bible studies to inform me of what was in the Bible. Then I joined a Bible study where the teacher challenged me to read Scripture. Just Scripture. No studies, no notes, just prayerfully approach Scripture and ask the Spirit to give me revelation. That's when Scripture came to life*

for me. That's when it became the living Word of God speaking to me and not just me reading words or filling in blanks. I desired to spend time with God through his Word and saw my faith mature and my love for God grow. The discipline of being in Scripture brought words of life to me daily. It was a beautiful time.

Then my church went through a crisis and I saw my brothers and sisters divide and hurt one another. I wanted to cling to the truth of Scripture and these were people I loved, but we were attacking each other. All kinds of sin reared its ugly head and many of us justified ourselves in it. This experience made me retreat. Not just from community, but from God, too. The pain of unrepentant sin made it easy to want to keep my distance from God and community. I would like to say it was a short time, but I'm stubborn.

Once despair began to set in, God, in His steadfast love, intervened, bringing to mind the truth of Scripture, and I slowly began to listen. It was a great time of back and forth with God, and he waited patiently for me. You see, I wanted to hold someone else accountable for their sin while I still hadn't repented of my own. God showed me in Scripture that Jesus' blood washes away the sin of all who believe in him. "This is the message we have heard from him and proclaim to you, that God is light, and in him is no darkness at all. If we say we have fellowship with him while we walk in darkness, we lie and do not practice the truth. But if we walk in the light, as he is in the light, we have fellowship with one another, and the blood of Jesus his Son cleanses us from all sin. If we say we have no sin, we deceive ourselves, and the truth is not in us. If we confess our sins, he is faithful and just to forgive us our sins and to cleanse us from all unrighteousness. If we say we have not sinned, we make him a liar, and his word in not in us." (1John 1:5-10) I literally got down on my knees and confessed my sin and experienced the washing away that only Jesus can do. I was then able to forgive those who had hurt me. God's truth, revealed in Scripture, brought me back into close relationship with Him and community. Praise be to God!

Julianna experienced what it was like to have sin—her own and someone else's—interrupt her time with God so that she began to let thoughts and feelings that weren't in line with God's standards crowd out the truth of how God wanted her to live. The remedy was to get back into God's Word so the truth could transform and heal.

If one problem is that we don't spend enough time with God to let Him influence us, we can choose to spend time with Him, listening and reading His Word. When we place ourselves in the position to hear God's unchanging and unfailing truth, He will speak His love, encouragement, and conviction to us through His Holy Spirit. Even when what we hear is challenging, we can trust it because it's spoken in love and it's true! And if we're hanging on to sin, cherishing it in our hearts, then we need to *stop, drop, and roll*.

Stop, Drop, and Roll

This is what we tell children to do in school if their clothes are on fire. Stop moving because you don't want to give the fire more oxygen. Drop to the ground. Then roll around to extinguish the flames. Sin is the same. We need to stop doing it. Stop going to the places and being with the people who bring out the worst in us. Stop feeding the flame of temptation or heartache. Then drop to our knees and confess and repent. Agree with God that what we've done is sin, turning around, away from it, asking Him for strength and direction to live differently. Finally, roll. Move on! The devil wants us to stay stuck in our sin. Sometimes it's the only thing he can do to keep us from being effective for God's kingdom. We're already saved and there's nothing the devil can do about it. But he will utilize every trick he can to paralyze us and make us quit trying.

I am fully convinced that God cares about obedience and holiness because He knows that by living obedient and holy lives we will be better off. His laws are for our provision and protection. I'm equally convinced that it's not a bad thing to hear God's Spirit tell us where we're out of line with His standards so He can change us. Our sin should wreck us because we're offending our loving Father who gave His Son as a redeeming sacrifice so that we can spend eternity with Him and enjoy life more fully here on earth. But our sin is also already paid for and that's the good news of the gospel! So we don't need to wallow, but we do need to acknowledge and repent.

When things are difficult or spiritually dissatisfying, we can intentionally participate in the transformation process. It's not that we're earning God's love or approval because He loved us perfectly and completely before we did anything impressive. We do what we can do: *listen, serve, submit, love* and *obey*. God does what only He can do: changes our hearts and speaks truth to us so we can shine.

> *His divine power has given us everything we need for a godly life through our knowledge of him who called us by his own glory and goodness. Through these he has given us his very great and precious promises, so that through them you may participate in the divine nature, having escaped the corruption in the world caused by evil desires.*
>
> (1 Peter 1:3-4)

We have everything we need to shine! Sin will show up as we burn off those outer layers of our previous lives, but God has given us the Holy Spirit as a deposit and a seal, reminding us that we're His and guaranteeing victory over sin as we trust Him to transform us into ever-increasing glory. We may burn out, flame out, and wipe out, but we will always come back to orbit around the God who made us and called us to shine.

Questions for Discussion or Application:

+ Do you most often feel disconnected, ignorant, or disobedient? What do you think God is asking you to change about your relationship with Him?

+ Read Psalm 139:23-24. Are you willing to make this your sincere prayer? If so, spend some time listening to God and write what you hear. If not, what is preventing you from it? Talk to God about it.

Chapter 6

Constellations

A constellation is a grouping of stars that form a pattern and are visible from the earth. When we lie on the grass or go to a planetarium, we see individual stars, but what helps us remember where they are is the fact that they're part of something bigger—a structure that gives their orbit and existence a framework. Constellations.

As we've explored the characteristics of stars, we've looked at some of their properties and how we can be similar to them as we grow in our spiritual journeys. Because stars can often be found in groupings in the sky, let's take some time to look at how to live out our lives shining as stars with each other. No star gets to shine alone in space and we are not supposed to live this Christian life alone, either.

A star is simply a burning ball of plasma, shining, burning, and being transformed. The same can be said of us as we shine brightly and uniquely in the world around us.

There are different kinds of stars in the universe and each category is based on size and where the star happens to be in its lifetime. Three of these stars are red dwarfs, yellow stars, and blue giants.

Red dwarf stars are the smallest. They are smaller than our sun and only burn a little fuel at a time because they are so small. They're not very hot, but they will burn for trillions of years.

Yellow stars, like our sun, are bigger than red dwarfs and burn their hydrogen cores faster and hotter. As they burn toward the end of their 10 billion-year life, they start to swell and engulf stars and planets around them. Finally, they shrink again and leave behind a cloud of gas called a planetary nebula.

Blue giants are very hot, very bright, and only live for about 100,000 years. They're the easiest to see from earth because they're so big, but they are rare. Unlike yellow stars, blue giants don't gently burn up and leave a pretty gas cloud behind; they explode into a super nova.

All of these stars shine and can be visible from Earth. All of them burn from their hydrogen core, emanating energy. They all continue in their unique orbits in space. The difference in them is in how they exist and for how long. Tiny, cool, and steady or huge, fiery, and explosive.

What if the three kinds of stars I described were people?

A red dwarf would be the kind of person who lives her life for God in a quiet way, serving people and loving them without much fanfare. She is a person with a healthy balance of connection to God and service to others, and she can go and go like the energizer bunny. This person may not get awards for spectacular achievements or garner a lot of recognition for her efforts, but she is pacing herself for a lifetime of service and she will have an impact on the people around her because she is faithful. Her energy burns steady, if not all that bright, but those closest to her can feel the warmth.

The downside to burning this low is that she can sometimes shy away from intense situations because she's used to a low glow. She may hesitate to give her opinion or speak up when she senses something is wrong because she doesn't want to make a big noise. She also may be easily intimidated by brighter and bigger stars who tend not to allow her light to be seen. She might need to be challenged to speak up and take risks once in a while.

A yellow star burns a little faster and a little hotter than the red dwarf. This star expands as it burns and will stop glowing at some point, becoming what astronomers call black stars. Our universe isn't old enough to have any, but that's what they'll be called some day. If planets are the right distance from yellow stars, life is possible because a yellow star gives the right amount of energy to sustain life.

Like a yellow star, we can sometimes be positive life-giving forces to those around us because of the energy we give off from our relationship with Christ. A yellow star will be a person with lots of people around her taking encouragement and comfort and getting energy from her light.

Because they burn hotter, yellow stars are also brighter and emanate light farther than a red dwarf. However, yellow stars have a tendency to expand and engulf all matter surrounding them. In the same way, a yellow star Christian needs to learn to use her energy for good and not evil as she recognizes the influence God has given her to the people around her. Luckily for her, if the yellow star keeps relying on God for her energy, even when she fails to see how she's eclipsing those around her, God's grace will surround her like a beautiful cloud, and He can still use her in the lives of others.

Blue giants are big and compact. They burn hot, hot, hot and they're huge. They can be seen for miles and miles but don't stick around long. Scientists use the location of blue giants to chart areas of space where new stars are being formed because they don't live long and tend to be in new areas.

Blue giants are risk-takers and can be found in adventurous scenarios with new people in new environments. Because they're hot, things and people around them can get burned, but they are ready and willing to light the way and blaze a new trail in life. They are the ones others watch and learn from. Because of their huge presence, they are hard to ignore for both good and bad reasons. They don't give much warning before they explode and they leave a huge path behind them to show where they've been. God can use the huge accomplishments and the huge blunders of blue giants to point others to Him, but the blue giant needs to remember to rely on God to lead the way.

So how do stars that are so different from each other come together to form something that is visible and organized from a distance? Ephesians 3:10-12 may give us some help.

> *His [God's] intent was that now, through the church, the manifold wisdom of God should be made known to the rulers and authorities in the heavenly realms, according to his eternal purpose which he accomplished in Christ Jesus our Lord. In him and through faith in him we may approach God with freedom and confidence.*

God's plan was that the church would show His glory and wisdom to the world. What is the church except a constellation of individual stars who are more recognizable together than they may be apart? This is community. We are not meant to live our lives as stars for Christ alone. There is greater value in pursuing God in all the ways we've talked about if we do it in community. God's intent was not that He would show the world and the heavenly realms all the aspects of His wisdom through individuals. His plan would be that His manifold—or many-faceted—wisdom would be evident as those individuals seek Him together.

Personal convictions and disciplines are important for us as individuals in that they feed the life of the community. ***Personal growth affects community.*** When I am healthy and connected to God's love and truth, I contribute healthy things to my community. When I'm not, I'll take from the community to fill what only God was meant to fill.

So even the activities on our star image are experienced individually, but fully manifest God's glory corporately.

Spending time listening to God, reading His Word, and confessing and repenting of our sins is crucial to our individual relationships with God AND to the life of our faith community specifically and generally.

I read the Bible every morning and I'm able to articulate God's truth in my life as the Holy Spirit reveals it to me. This allows me to say no to temptation, to become more aware of others as I serve them, and to love and obey God more completely as He reveals His will to me while I listen to Him. That's a beautiful benefit to my placing myself in a position to listen to God and spend time with Him. He convicts me of my sin, refines my character, and frees me from lies so I can walk in the freedom of the truth.

But that kind of transformation doesn't happen in a vacuum. I am in constant relationship with others. If God tells me to serve, whom do I serve if not those around me? If God convicts me of sin, is it not generally because I've hurt someone I'm in relationship with?

Conversely, our experiences within the community of faith can have a powerful impact on how we relate to God individually, as well. When we first discovered that Charlie was using drugs, there were times when I didn't know how to pray for him or for us. I felt like all I could do was lift up my hands to God and cry out. There was a woman at church whose faith was much bigger than mine and who could pray the things I wish I had the strength and clarity to pray myself. One Sunday I went to the front of the sanctuary after the service, seeking her out. My plan was to simply ask if she would pray for our family. I didn't get two words out before the tears came. She grabbed both my hands firmly in hers and started praying up a storm! She reminded God that He's the one who calls things into being that aren't. She prayed for Charlie to become a man who loves God and tells others about Him. She prayed and prayed, and I nodded and cried. "Yes, Lord!" was all I could say.

Later, when I would spend time in Scripture, reading and praying for Charlie, I recalled some of the verses my friend had prayed, and I prayed them, too. And it encouraged me to find other verses to pray. All because I had been lifted up and encouraged by her faith when my had faltered.

Living in community means that we will reap the benefits of having others in our lives, and we will also experience the friction that those relationships bring.

Here are just some of the most wonderful aspects of community:

* We see aspects of God's character that we don't see alone.

* We support one another when things are difficult.

* We can experience God's forgiveness through others.

* We hold each other accountable to growth and truth based on God's Word.

* Our gifts and experiences complement one another so the world sees more of who God is.

However, haven't we also experienced the negative effects of someone else's sin spilling into our lives, being forced to spend time with and forgive people we don't like, and adjusting to others as their growth chart looks very different from ours? This, too, is part of church life. God can use these situations to challenge us to depend more fully on Him. When faced with some of the unpleasantness of life in community, we need to reread practical sections of Scripture that remind us of the character we're meant to develop. It's also imperative that we pray sincerely for God to change our hearts. He's the only one who can.

There are areas of sin to be dealt with in community, but there are also areas where we are to extend grace. To let people live out their own relationships with God. I have tried to be a Holy Spirit to people, and I'm terrible at it! We can and should hold each other accountable to God's commandments in the Bible, reminding one another of the truth in love. But there are some areas in which only God can tell us how to live. We only answer to him, so it's wise to distinguish between sin issues and what the Bible calls "disputable matters" (Romans 14).

In 1 Corinthians 5, Paul rebukes the readers for condoning a man's sexual relationship with his stepmother. Jude writes about *"godless men, who change the grace of our God into a license for immorality and deny Jesus Christ our only Sovereign and Lord"* (Jude 4). These are areas of concern for the integrity of doctrine and the health of community; the truth of the gospel must be preserved.

However, there are other areas of preference or individual conviction, and these are left to each believer to identify and live out according to how God's Spirit directs. Among these disputable matters are issues of parenting, movie and music choices, nutrition, communication styles, and career paths. These are also some of the issues that provide opportunities for us to grow in our faith as we examine our own beliefs and release others to make their own choices.

It's all part of being in a constellation, but it's all meant to show the world how awesome our God is!

Look at this passage, which describes the combination of individual and corporate spiritual life:

Brothers, if someone is caught in a sin, you who are spiritual should restore him gently. But watch yourself, or you also may be tempted. Carry each other's burdens, and in this way you will fulfill the law of Christ. If anyone thinks he is something when he is nothing, he deceives himself. Each one should test his own actions. Then he can take pride in himself, without comparing himself to somebody else, for each one should carry his own load.

(Galatians 6:1-5)

This is a great picture of a balance between pursuing God individually and taking part in that transformation process, while also allowing ourselves to be influenced by others in the constellation. There is accountability, love, and cooperation in this passage. That's how we show the world what God looks like. By restoring each other instead of judging because we know how hard it is to walk this journey. By taking responsibility for our own spiritual journey instead of depending on the pastor or leaders in the church to "feed us." By standing firm in our individual relationship with Jesus so we don't suffer and hurt relationships by comparing ourselves to others. Isn't that a place you want to be? I do. Where my obedience and my love for God encourage you in your obedience. When it's hard for you, I'll help. And when it's hard for me, I hope you'll do the same. In the meantime, we each have our own journeys to walk. Journeys of love, submission, listening, obedience, and service.

Then we pour out what we've learned into the lives of others:

I long to see you so that I may impart to you some spiritual gifts to make you strong—that is, that you and I may be mutually encouraged by each other's faith.

(Romans 1:11-12)

Let us therefore make every effort to do what leads to peace and to mutual edification.

(Romans 14:19)

I invite you to speak truth into my life and I'll speak truth into yours, but how can either of us speak that truth if we don't spend time reading and listening to learn it in the first place? And how exactly should we mutually edify each other and impart spiritual gifts to make each other strong?

One effective way of doing this is discipleship.

Discipleship

Those who are older and more experienced with spiritual matters are meant to be sharing those experiences and truths with others in the community. Paul wrote to Titus and told him to "teach sound doctrine" in the church. He warned him against those who might wreck families with false teaching. He encouraged him to set an example for the community in the way he led his life, with integrity and good works, giving no reason for others to question his authority or sincerity. And he told Titus to teach the older women how to reflect the character of God so that *"they can train the younger women"* (Titus 1-2).

Paul's 2nd letter to the Corinthians reminded believers that they are meant to comfort others with the comfort they themselves have received from God.

Community can reflect God's manifold wisdom when we intentionally invest in one another to teach sound doctrine and flesh out God's character and glory for the world. Then we will shine like stars in the crooked and perverse generation we live in. And as we invest in newer believers, we help them grow and know the truth they're learning in the hopes that they will pass it along to others in the future. Jesus did it with his 12 disciples. Paul wrote letters to the men he discipled. It's part of being in a healthy, growing community.

Who should be a part of this process? Well, everyone in some way, but here are some guidelines indicating that you might be ready to take on the responsibility of investing in another woman in a mentor relationship.

Relationship with Christ—Have you accepted Jesus as the only payment for your sin and the only way to get to heaven to spend eternity with God? Do you love Him and have you committed to follow Him with your whole heart for your whole life? That's key.

Regular intake of Scripture—I'm not talking about reading just for Bible study, but to hear from God on your own on a regular basis. Have you read the whole Bible? Do you hear God when you read? Does the Holy Spirit guide you, convict you, and help you grow as you know more and more of God's Word?

Growing Prayer Life—This doesn't have to mean that you have a prayer closet like in the movie *War Room* but it does mean that you understand and engage in prayer differently and more profoundly than you used to. Is God changing your heart so that you pray for yourself and others more than you used to?

Humility—When you read the Bible and when you listen to God in prayer, are you prepared to obey what the Spirit reveals to you? Do you rely on the Holy Spirit to speak truth and love others well?

Mentor—Ideally, you should have someone who is discipling you in your life! What we receive and learn we pass along to others. Psalm 101:6 says,

> *My eyes will be on the faithful in the land,*
> *that they may dwell with me;*
> *the one whose walk is blameless*
> *will minister to me.*

We can actively look for those who can show us what it looks like to pattern our lives after God in various areas, and then we emulate that and pass it along to others.

This process may be a formal one or situational—long-term or short-term. The important thing is to be looking for opportunities and praying for the wisdom to enter into them effectively. Wherever you may be in your spiritual journey, there will always be someone with less knowledge and experience. There will also always be someone with more. It's a great place to be, being challenged and encouraged to shine like a star!

Let me share with you some principles that have been helpful to me recently as I've been thinking about the relationships I've had with newer believers and younger women over the years.

Read this passage from the book of Acts:

> *Now an angel of the Lord said to Philip, "Go south to the road—the desert road—that goes down from Jerusalem to Gaza." So he started out, and on his way he met an Ethiopian eunuch, an important official in charge of all the treasury of the Kandake (which means 'queen of the Ethiopians'). This man had gone to Jerusalem to worship, and on his way home was sitting in his chariot reading the Book of Isaiah the prophet. The Spirit told Philip, "Go to that chariot and stay near it."*
>
> *Then Philip ran up to the chariot and heard the man reading Isaiah the prophet. "Do you understand what you are reading?" Philip asked.*
>
> *"How can I," he said, "unless someone explains it to me?" So he invited Philip to come up and sit with him.*
>
> *This is the passage of Scripture the eunuch was reading:*
> *"He was led like a sheep to the slaughter,*
> *and as a lamb before its shearer is silent,*
> *so he did not open his mouth.*
> *In his humiliation he was deprived of justice.*
> *Who can speak of his descendants?*
> *For his life was taken from the earth."*
>
> *The eunuch asked Philip, "Tell me, please, who is the prophet talking about, himself or someone else?" Then Philip began with that very passage of Scripture and told him the good news about Jesus.*
>
> *As they traveled along the road, they came to some water and the eunuch said, "Look, here is water. What can stand in the way of my being baptized?" And he gave orders to stop the chariot. Then both Philip and the eunuch went down into the water and Philip baptized him. When they came up out of the water, the Spirit of the Lord suddenly took Philip away, and the eunuch did not see him again, but went on his way rejoicing. Philip, however, appeared at Azotus and traveled about, preaching the gospel in all the towns until he reached Caesarea.* (Acts 8:26-40)

Here are the principles that have been encouraging to me:

1) **Be ready and available.** Follow God's instruction one step at a time when it comes to relationships. If you feel a prompting by the Holy Spirit to spend time with someone intentionally, do it, especially if she is younger in her faith than you are or new to your community. Philip was just told which road and which direction to go down. Not the end destination or what would happen along the way. The Bible is full of stories like this. We just need to start with the top of the star: **LISTEN.**

2) **Stand by the chariot.** We don't know what someone may be learning or struggling with in their spiritual journeys, so we need to start by just being near enough to learn something about each person we might start spending time with. Philip obeyed God's direction to start going down the road, then very specifically was ready to obey when he was told to stand by the chariot, not knowing who was inside or what would happen. We don't know what God is doing in others' lives if we don't stand by their chariot to participate in the process. And notice that Philip wasn't just going through the motions of obedience. Acts 8:30 says, "Philip RAN..."

3) **Ask questions.** To effectively disciple someone, we need to know what God's been up to and what questions our new friend may have. And notice that Philip and the Ethiopian eunuch start talking about Scripture. Wherever the women we disciple happen be, our job is to meet them there and lead them to Jesus. By asking questions Philip knew to start with Isaiah and connect it to Jesus. That leads to my next observation.

4) **Know Scripture.** This is a perfect example of how our individual discipline of spending time with God and learning His Word plays itself out in community. What God teaches me, I pass along to others. Imagine how differently the conversation between Philip and the Ethiopian would have been if Philip had answered, "Isaiah...I know I've read that. It's in the Old Testament, right?" Instead, Philip was not only familiar with the passage the eunuch was reading, but he also knew how to connect it to the saving

message of the gospel of Jesus! You don't have to know everything, but if we truly believe that *all* Scripture is God-breathed and useful for correcting, rebuking, and training in righteousness (2 Timothy 3:16-17), we need to know what's in there to pass it along!

5) **Encourage them to obey.** When the Ethiopian saw water, the next step in his spiritual development became clear: baptism. Jesus told the disciples to, *"go and make disciples of all nations, baptizing them in the name of the Father and of the Son and of the Holy Spirit, and teaching them to obey everything I have commanded you"* (Matt 28:19-20). Discipleship in community is more than just getting someone to say a prayer so they go to heaven instead of hell. It's also about teaching them to obey and the satisfaction that comes from that. Baptism is a great example of that. Jesus was baptized, and if it was important to Him, it should be important to us. We teach others to obey by modeling obedience in all areas of life.

6) **Hold things loosely.** After the eunuch's baptism, Philip was taken away and the two men never met again. It was a discipleship relationship for a short season. That may be the case with us, and it doesn't mean we've done something wrong or that God is done using us. As long as you have breath in your body, God is not done using you! But when my discipleship relationships would come to an end after a season, I used to wonder if it was because I wasn't being effective or because they didn't like me or because of some other reason. Recently God has revealed to me that it may just be time to move on. God does what only He can do, and He calls me to be obedient to what He calls me to do.

I've had a few experiences of meeting with college-age women to talk about the Bible and life and whatever comes up. I've always enjoyed the question/answer part of the relationship and how vulnerable young women can be when we talk about spiritual matters. When the college years were over, however, even though they stayed around, the relationship changed dramatically. I told the women at that point that I would leave things up to them—if they want to continue to meet regularly or sporadically, it's totally up to them. And I don't meet with any of them anymore. I stood by the chariot and then God told me to move on.

Other discipleship relationships have turned into friendships and I still hang out with women I've met in Bible studies I've led. My friend Julianna and I joke about the summer years ago when we decided to study the book of Daniel together only to discover that we talked almost exclusively about marriage when we got together. Who knew the book of Daniel could speak life into our marriages? We started as a mentor/disciple relationship and became best friends.

Currently, I meet twice a month with Carolyn, who works for a non-profit organization in Seattle that helps women escape from the sex trade. Because I have done some work with nonprofit fundraising as an auctioneer and MC, I'm able to guide her both professionally and spiritually when we meet together. I'm old enough to be her mom, but we have developed a lovely comradery and we both benefit from our time together.

Here is what she says about the process we've enjoyed together:

> *The mentoring process is like having a gentle, but knowing pair of hands guiding me along the ever-winding pathway of life. It's like tapping into decades of wisdom that I haven't earned yet and letting that maturity speak into the personal, professional, and spiritual spaces of my life.*
>
> *I've found that community with peers in similar life stages is critical so we can encourage each other in the challenges we're facing, but having a mentor, who's likely already scaled those mountains and navigated the valleys, opens up a wealth of wisdom from someone who has been there before. It's a safe space to bring hard questions, air questionable choices, and to seek accountability.*
>
> *For me, spending intentional time with a confident, bold woman who owns her swagger simply because she knows who she is has been transformative for me. I've spent years of my life trying to imitate others, but this relationship empowers me to live from an authentic space and walk boldly in the freedom I was created for.*
>
> *This boldness I'm cultivating spills into my other relationships, where I now have a clearer vision of who I want around me, speaking into my life, and into my behaviors and beliefs, because I'm more trusting in*

God's goodness the more I study his character.

Having accountability in my walk with Jesus has been a game-changer. Regular check-ins and conversations about what I'm reading help me develop this spiritual discipline and influences how I view God.

If you don't have a gray-haired person who has access to your life, you're missing out on one of life's richest experiences.

If you are a mature believer, I can't encourage you strongly enough to make yourself available to younger women who haven't yet learned and grown in the same ways that you have. If you are a newer believer or a young woman who wants to learn more about how to navigate life with faith as your guide, watch the women around you and see how they imitate Jesus. Whether the time is informal, for a brief season, or part of a long-term and structured set-up, both the woman doing the spiritual investing and the one receiving wisdom will benefit from some level of intergenerational interaction.

In the time I've spent discipling women over the years, I have discovered and developed some resources that I have found to be very helpful. Some of these resources are included here. Others are worth searching out in a bookstore or online, since it's easier to have some sort of structure to alter than it is to begin each time you spend together from scratch. It's important to remember that the frequency and content of your time together can be whatever God leads you to create. There is no set pattern for how time is structured, whether it's formal Bible study, chatting over coffee, or a fitness/spiritual development combo. We just need to connect what God is doing in us individually to what God is doing in community, because, *"Those who are wise will shine like the brightness of the heavens, and those who lead many to righteousness, like the stars for ever and ever"* (Daniel 12:3).

We are all part of the constellation of God's people, equipped and commanded to shine brightly TOGETHER in community.

Discipleship isn't the only way to shine in a spiritual constellation, however. There are many aspects of doing life together that will achieve the same purpose in the universe. It might be easier to think of the larger constellations idea if we boil it down three ways I think we're called to live in community: *Bear, Share*, and *Care*.

Bear:

* *Fruit that will last (John 15:16)* We're not just adding numbers to a congregation or making sure people say the "Sinner's Prayer." Bearing fruit that will last involves long-term relationships that are transparent and growing in godliness and affecting the world around us in kingdom ways. Heart change leads to changes in behavior that reveal God's love to the world around us.

* *With the failings of the weak (Romans 15:1)* We grow in different ways and at different rates. We stick to sound doctrine in "spine issues" but give grace for specific areas of conviction in "rib issues."

* *With each other (Colossians 3:13)* God calls us to forgive and extend grace to others in community. It's what He did for us so when we experience it together, we're reminded of God's larger, perfect qualities.

* *Each other's burdens (Galatians 6:2)* We carry the load for each other when things are difficult. This may be preparing or serving meals for someone who's grieving or overwhelmed. It may mean listening once more to a story of struggle when a friend is processing great change in her life. It can look like taking on extra ministry responsibilities when someone is in a particularly challenging season of life.

Share:

* *Resources (Romans 12:13; Hebrews 13:16)* When community members are called to go on a mission trip, we give. When someone loses a job, we help financially. Visiting pastors or speakers may need a place to stay; those with the gift of hospitality chomp at the bit to share resources this way! We tithe obediently to help the church reach those who haven't heard of God's love or those who are hurting or in crisis.

* *Our faith and experiences (Philemon 1:6)* One of the greatest disservices that seasoned believers commit is not allowing others to hear the tales of their triumphs AND defeats as they've walked with Jesus. I absolutely love hearing my girlfriends recount stories about how God has spoken to them through Scripture or in family situations, convicting them of sin and revealing new aspects of Himself. And they're recent experiences, too, not something that happened in college decades ago. We are called to keep our individual encounters with God fresh and dynamic and to share those experiences with others in community. This is how we flesh out more and more of God's character to teach and encourage one another.

* *Suffering and glory (Romans 8:17)* We remind each other of the inheritance we share in Christ, which includes suffering AND glory. And beyond simply reminding one another of the suffering and glory we're destined for as we commit to following Christ, we walk together in the suffering and witness the glory as our lives are transformed.

* *NOT in others' sins* (1 Timothy 5:22) We come alongside each other and speak truth and extend grace, but we do NOT share in behavior or attitudes that go against Scripture or the conviction of the Holy Spirit. There's a fine line between walking with someone who is struggling to find victory in some area of sin and veering off the straight and narrow to go down the path of destruction with them out of some sense of solidarity or support. When we are grounded in the truth of Scripture, sure of our center of gravity, we can orbit among the debris while still maintaining our own values and pursuit of holiness.

Care:

* *By investing in others' spiritual growth* (2 Timothy 2:2; Titus 2:3-5) Paul told Titus to *"teach the older women to be reverent in the way they live...to teach what is good. Then they can train the younger women...so that no one will malign the word of God"* (Titus 2:3-5). His instructions to Timothy toward the men in community were similar: *"... the things you have heard me say in the presence of many*

witnesses entrust to reliable men who will also be qualified to teach others" (2 Timothy 2:2). We show that we care about individuals and community life by making the effort to invest in one another spiritually.

* *By teaching / living sound doctrine* (1 Timothy 1:3-7) We show that we love each other by teaching and showing by example that we are pursuing Christ. Love, a pure heart, a good conscience, and sincere faith are the motivating factors leading us to stay true to sound doctrine in our own lives so that new believers and younger people have models for what passionate pursuit of godliness looks like. Allowing false doctrine and lackadaisical spiritual activities shows that we don't care very deeply about each other or about our own relationship with God.

* *Physical needs* (Luke 10:34; Matthew 25:31-40) Jesus' example to us was to take care of each other when we are sick, hungry, and in need. When we serve "the least of these" we are demonstrating how much we care about following Jesus and about those He has called us to love in the world.

* *For each other* (John 21:16) If we love Jesus, we will take care of His people. Jesus' post-resurrection encounter with Peter reveals His heart for those of us who would also follow Him: *Take care of my sheep.*

The Rhythm of Community

Let me wrap up this section with something that has occurred to me recently as my husband and I are about to celebrate our 25th wedding anniversary. Many of those years have been challenging. There have been times when we were both tempted to call it quits and times when we knew we were white-knuckling it through. Sometimes the difficult seasons were circumstantial, like grieving the death of a sibling or a parent, living through cancer treatments with Charlie, or the pain and loneliness of having sent our only child to rehab. Like many of you, we have also had our share of financial strain, professional struggles, and household stress (plumbing!). Other times the stress was due to personal inner turmoil or misunderstandings between us. I've doubted my purpose and have been hurt by my own sin as well as others', and Tony has his own catalogue of internal dialogues with himself and with God that have silenced him because of shame and anger. In the midst of these struggles we have also had wonderful and lengthy seasons of celebration, peace, passion, and adventure, and we are on a more solid and loving foundation than when we took our vows.

In our own marriage and in dozens of stories I could tell you, I have seen a pattern emerge over and over again that seems to be a watershed for relationships: involvement in community.

I don't think, as Tony and I reflect over our 25 years of marriage, that I can overestimate the importance of our Sunday rhythm. There have been countless Sundays when we have left for church with our shoulders tight, our breathing shallow, and our brows furrowed because of the weight of our internal struggles or external pressures, only to hear truth spoken in a message that causes us to pour our hearts out to God in worshipful response so that our bodies and souls sigh deeply in spiritual recalibration. Taking our individual heart issues into the healing environment of community, where we corporately are reminded of a much bigger perspective and where we surrender to God's truth, mystery, and grace, allows us to turn toward each other instead of remaining in a silo of pain, wallowing in silent lies and recriminations or lashing out at each other to accuse and malign. Being in community, week after week, year after year, doing life together with like-minded Christ-followers, serves as a sort of spiritual and social touchstone to support and encourage us to pursue God's standards and reflect His love to one another.

When circumstances or intentional choices lead us away from being part of a community of faith on a regular basis—in a rhythm that characterizes our lives—our marriages become more vulnerable to competing affections, personal overindulgence, and straying from the truth of who we know God to be and who He says we are. This vulnerability can lead to compromising and slacking in other areas, as well, and it is far more difficult to then maintain a Christian marriage that shines to the world like the stars we're supposed to be. "Taking time off" from going to church may be the impetus needed to start down a variety of slippery slopes in life including:

* **Not teaching children about God or taking them to church.** This results in an entire generation of children who will need to hear the gospel for the first time and undo the world's standards because they haven't learned God's. They may also choose friends differently, engage in activities that seem acceptable by society's standards but are not beneficial for them from God's perspective, and struggle with character issues. These things are by no means guaranteed to be a breeze if we are part of a community of faith, but by *not* surrounding ourselves with others who can challenge and encourage us to follow God, we relinquish the most influential years we have as parents to provide a foundation that will become a part of their spiritual DNA as adults, even if they stray from it for a season. In community, we are reminded that God alone holds the future of our children, and we are encouraged to look to Him, pray to Him, and trust in Him alone to save them and make them thrive.

* **Engaging in inappropriate relationships with men who are not our husbands.** Without anyone around to remind us of God's truth on a regular basis (weekly, at least!), we are more susceptible to rationalizing business lunches, flirting, and more with other men. Not many Christian women purpose to let their faith and community fall away so that they can slowly let their marriages die and have affairs or get divorced. But incremental steps away from community can lead to unintended consequences for the most well-intentioned among us. Listening to God's truth being spoken every week, surrounded by others who are focused on loving, serving, and obeying God and others, centers us and allows us to see and love our husbands the way God intends.

* **Becoming bad ambassadors for Christ.** Because the church is God's vehicle for reflecting His wisdom, love, and glory to the world, we are shining less brightly by removing ourselves from the constellation. I can't possibly reflect all the best of God's character to the world; I need the whole body of Christ to do that! When I remove myself from all community, I allow the church to show the world a less accurate picture of God's family. And alone, without complementary parts of the body in my life, I'm showing the world a woefully inadequate image of my loving Father.

Please don't misunderstand what I'm saying to mean that taking a few weeks away from church to go on vacation or take a much-needed rest is going to ruin your marriage or your family. What I do find to be true over and over again is that "taking a break" from church turns into, "We don't go to church anymore." Going to church on Sundays is not a promise of conjugal bliss, but removing ourselves from a healthy source of grace and truth might contribute to relational distance in a marriage. And if Christian marriage is meant to reflect the mystery of Christ and the church, we will need all the help we can get to do it right!

If you are a Christian woman married to a man who doesn't come to church with you or who isn't a believer, you need the rhythm of community every bit as much as women married to Christian men. You, however, will be faced with a challenge of how to spend time with people who will speak truth to you and encourage and love you to be the best wife you can be to your husband. You will need to also be sensitive to time spent with your husband doing things outside the community of faith so that church doesn't become a wedge between you. I've seen church activity and even Bible reading cause tension between spouses who aren't on the same spiritual page. My encouragement to you is to prioritize friendships with women who are passionately and consistently pursuing God through corporate worship and individual time in Scripture. That way they can remind you of how much God loves you and how He wants you to listen, serve, submit, love and obey so you can shine with joy in precisely the way He created you to shine!

Regardless of our marital status or spiritual and relationship struggles, community is crucial in stabilizing and enriching our personal journeys. However, we must never let community spiritual experience replace the personal experience. We reflect God's beauty in a dark universe because we're part of His constellation family, but we are loved for who we are individually. He speaks to us individually, and we are meant to shine for Him uniquely, just the way He made us.

We bear, share, and care in our constellations so we can shine like stars as we hold out the word of life to a crooked and warped generation.

Questions for Discussion or Application:

+ Where have you seen examples of community done well?

+ In what ways do you see a connection between your personal spiritual growth and community life?

+ What parts of life in a community of faith do you find particularly rewarding? Challenging?

+ How are you currently involved in a discipleship relationship? If you aren't, how could you be?

Conclusion:

Burn From Within

Stars burn from within. The nuclear fusion that takes place at the hydrogen core of a star emanates outward. Since hydrogen is the most plentiful gas in space, as it burns at the core of a star, heat can continue to emanate from that core for millions or billions of years. In the same way, John 3:34 says that *"God gives the Spirit without limit."* One of our most confident prayers for ourselves and for others can be to ask God for more and more of His Spirit. And as we read prayers of the saints in Scripture who have gone before us, we can grow in our passion for God and for others and ask God to do in us what they asked Him to do in them. What a great place to look when we don't know how to pray!

Look at how a prayer in Ephesians could fuel us to shine brightly in the world even though Paul prayed it for fellow believers 2000 years ago.

> *I keep asking that the God of our Lord Jesus Christ, the glorious Father, may give you the Spirit of wisdom and revelation, so that you may know him better. I pray that the eyes of your heart may be enlightened in order that you may know the hope to which he has called you, the riches of his glorious inheritance in his holy people, and his incomparably great power for us who believe. That power is the same as the mighty strength he exerted when he raised Christ from the dead and seated him at his right hand in the heavenly realms, far above all rule and authority, power and dominion, and every name that is invoked, not only in the present age but also in the one to come.*

> (Ephesians 1:17-21)

Who in our lives wouldn't love having this prayed for them? It's easy to apply this to individuals in our lives as the Holy Spirit brings them to mind. Watch how I change Paul's prayer to one for a friend:

Glorious Father, I'm going to keep asking you over and over again to give Jessica the Spirit of wisdom and revelation so that she might know you better. Would you enlighten the eyes of her heart—that spiritual part of her that doesn't see you and sense you right now—so she would know what hope in you feels like. You have given us great power in our lives—power that raises the dead! Would she sense that power and that hope in her current situation in her relationships, remembering that you are above all her circumstances and are fully in control. Give her your perspective and fill her with confidence and hope in the name of Jesus. Amen.

If we have the right motivation and relationship with God inside our spirits, we will burn with passion for Him over the course of our lives and people will see it. That Spirit will fuel us until the very end of our lives so that instead of becoming a dense black hole that sucks the energy out of people and situations, we will bring life and light into the rooms we enter because we know who we are, what we believe, and we are compelled by a loving and powerful God to share His truth and love with those around us.

What does Paul refer to when he encourages believers to shine like stars as the *"hold firmly to the word of life?"* What is this word that we're meant to be holding as we shine? What external effect will there be to this internal burning of the Holy Spirit?

Paul is encouraging the Philippian Christians—and us—to hold out the gospel. To hold out the hopeful message of redemption that Jesus' life, death, and resurrection display. And when we shine as a star in a dark and crooked world, we are holding out hope. Showing people what a life orbiting around Jesus looks like.

Merely reading and understanding the Bible isn't shining. Obedience alone isn't necessarily shining. But letting God's Spirit transform us so that we don't conform to the rest of the world shines! The difference in how we speak, how we respect others, how we spend our money and our time... these are things that shine to those without the hope of Jesus to light up the darkness around them.

We can read about tithing in the Bible. We can understand the concept of generosity and acknowledge it as God's standard. The Holy Spirit will move in us to change our understanding AND our behavior until we find that giving is more natural than it was previously. God will take the money we've given in obedience and use it for His kingdom. That is how He operates. But that shines like a star when a CPA looks at an income tax return and says, "Wow! You give a lot of money away!" That looks different from the rest of the world and that difference shines!

When a woman owns a clothing boutique and balances family, professional, and church aspects of her life well, that's impressive, but it's not necessarily shining. However, when she uses her business and her background in fashion merchandising to make women feel valued, and when she takes every opportunity to recount her testimony to clients so they can hear how God has healed her from cancer and helped her start her business, she is holding out the word of life, giving hope to women who listen. That's shining!

We shine by knowing what God says about who we are and how to live. Then we put it into action in front of the people around us.

In a period of history when natural disasters devastate lives, mass shootings are commonplace, and pornographic publishers like Hugh Hefner are lauded as industry pioneers instead of the depraved and selfish entrepreneurs they really are, shining light into a dark world is critical. Paul reminded the Thessalonian Christians that the gospel came to them *not simply with words, but also with power, with the Holy Spirit and with deep conviction*" (1 Thessalonians 1:5). That conviction and power propels us into the world to love and live differently. It takes a limitless resource like God's Holy Spirit and keeps fusing it and fusing it deep in our cores to create love, light, and truth that emanates from us into the dark, crooked, depraved, and lost world.

The apostle John reminded us of Jesus' words: *"If you hold to my teaching, you are really my disciples. Then you will know the truth, and the truth will set you free"* (John 8:31-32). And in his later letter, he said, *"...you have an anointing from the Holy One, and all of you know the truth"* (1 John 2:20). There is freedom in knowing God and in knowing His word. We can't experience the freedom of deeply held convictions that allow us to go out boldly into the world unless we know the truth of where it comes from: the Bible itself. But once we do, watch out, world!

But what if you don't have the desire to read the Bible? What if you don't know where to begin? The desire for anything good comes from God alone. He is at work in us and He is sovereign over our hearts, so the place to start is by asking Him to *give* us the desire to read His Word so that we can learn and implement it. John Piper's perspective is helpful as he gives an example prayer, exemplifying the urgency and radical nature of praying for the kind of desire that necessitates humility and surrender to His will:

> *O God, for Christ's sake! For the sake of your dear Son! For the sake of his infinitely precious blood (1 Peter 1:19), hear my cry and restore to me the joy of my salvation (Psalm 51:12) and the delight I once had in your word (Psalm 1:2). Restore to me the fullness of my love for you (Deuteronomy 30:6). Grant me to say again from the bottom of my heart, "Oh, how I love your law!" (Psalm 119:97).*[1]

God is faithful and He longs for us to long for Him. As He reveals Himself in His Word, we have a more complete and profound understanding of who He is and who we are. This is where our identity and confidence come from so we can shine in the generation to which we are called.

As we end our discussion together, I want to leave you with some sections of Scripture that are both encouraging and right in line with all we've explored. Use them as a reminder of things in the previous chapters, or simply read them and pray for yourself or someone you know. As I've written this book, I have prayed that God would use it to bring women closer to Him and to impact the world for His glory. Wherever you are, in whatever season of life, shine, sister, shine!

We continually ask God to fill you with the knowledge of his will through all the wisdom and understanding that the Spirit gives, so that you may live a life worthy of the Lord and please him in every way: bearing fruit in every good work, growing in the knowledge of God, being strengthened with all power according to his glorious might so that you may have great endurance and patience, and giving joyful thanks to the Father, who has qualified you to share in the inheritance of his holy people in the kingdom of light. For he has rescued us from the dominion of darkness and brought us into the kingdom of the Son he loves, in whom we have redemption, the forgiveness of sins.

(Colossians 1:9-13)

May the Lord make your love increase and overflow for each other and for everyone else, just as ours does for you. May he strengthen your hearts so that you will be blameless and holy in the presence of our God and Father when our Lord Jesus comes with all his holy ones.

(1 Thessalonians 3:12-13)

May our Lord Jesus Christ himself and God our Father, who loved us and by his grace gave us eternal encouragement and good hope, encourage your hearts and strengthen you in every good deed and word.

(2 Thessalonians 2:16-17)

Now may the God of peace who brought again from the dead our Lord Jesus, the great shepherd of the sheep, by the blood of the eternal covenant, equip you with everything good that you may do his will, working in us that which is pleasing in his sight, through Jesus Christ, to whom be glory forever and ever. Amen.

(Hebrews 13:20-21)

Endnotes

Introduction

1 Köstenberger, Andreas J. and Patterson, Richard D. *Invitation to Biblical Interpretation*: *Exploring the Hermeneutical Triad of History, Literature, and Theology*. Grand Rapids: Kregel, 2011.

Chapter 1

1 http://www.skyandtelescope.com/astronomy-resources/what-is-a-star/

2 Piper, John. *Reading the Bible Supernaturally, Seeing and Savoring the Glory of God in Scripture*. Crossway, 2017

Chapter 2

1 Eastman, Dick. *The Hour That Changes the World*. Chosen Books, Anniversary edition, 2002

2 Scott, Susan. *Fierce Conversations: Achieving Success at Work and in Life One Conversation at a Time*. Penguin Group / Viking Studio, 2002

3 http://www.myersbriggs.org/my-mbti-personality-type/mbti-basics/

4 http://strengths.gallup.com/110440/About-StrengthsFinder-20.aspx

5 Butts, Jessica. *Live Your Life from the Front Seat*. LegacyOne Authors, 2015

Chapter 4

1 http://www.atnf.csiro.au/outreach/education/senior/astrophysics/binary_intro.html

Chapter 5

1 https://www.space.com/38057-sun-unleashes-decades-strongest-solar-flare.html

2 https://www.nasa.gov/mission_pages/swift/bursts/monster_flare.html

Conclusion

1 Piper, John. *Reading the Bible Supernaturally, Seeing and Savoring the Glory of God in Scripture*. Crossway, 2017

A FORMER HIGH SCHOOL French and English teacher, Jenni Butz now employs her dynamic energy and honed communication skills to entertain, organize, and inform, while unpacking some of life's more challenging lessons with an authentic and humorous twist. A firm believer that God's Word is active, practical, and relevant for all people in all seasons of life, Jenni speaks to women's groups in church and corporate settings, and she is particularly passionate about intentional sleepovers (otherwise known as retreat weekends). She also works as MC and auctioneer for nonprofit fundraising in the Pacific Northwest, where she lives with her husband.

www.ingramcontent.com/pod-product-compliance
Lightning Source LLC
Chambersburg PA
CBHW060054100426
42742CB00014B/2827